Sidney Paine Johnston

The Manual of Receipts

Being a Collection of Formulæ and Process for Artisans

Sidney Paine Johnston

The Manual of Receipts
Being a Collection of Formulæ and Process for Artisans

ISBN/EAN: 9783337217891

Printed in Europe, USA, Canada, Australia, Japan

Cover: Foto ©Suzi / pixelio.de

More available books at **www.hansebooks.com**

IMPORTANT.

We would have you notice that the world is moving—moving rapidly, too. Rapid advances have been made in all kinds of business operations during the last decade, and in none more than in the Stove and Furnace business. Just here we would whisper in confidence to you, that this rapid advance, so far as the stove business is concerned, has not been an universal one. There are still some back numbers in the business—men who think "a stove good enough for **GRANDFATHER** is good enough for me." Now, we feel sure you are not to be classed among that number; in fact, we **KNOW** you are not one of that class, otherwise you would not be reading this book. Now, then, knowing you to be a live, progressive, wide-awake dealer, we feel no hesitancy whatever in stating clearly and plainly, so as not to be misunderstood, that if you desire to keep your reputation of progressiveness, as well as your growing trade, you cannot afford to overlook our line of strictly up-to-date stoves and furnaces. Of course, we cannot enumerate them all here, but can only call your attention to our line of Penn Esther Ranges. They are the leading ranges on the market to-day. We make that assertion without fear of contradiction—it is an acknowledged fact. They are selling as fast as we can make them, and if you want to be in it, you cannot afford to do business without having them represented on your floor.

The same can be said of our Penn Perfect Furnace—but in order to appreciate our line you should be in possession of our latest catalogue, circulars, etc., and a postal card will procure them. Remember that the Mt. Penn Stove Works, located at Reading, Pennsylvania, is moving—moving rapidly, as we stated the world was, at the beginning of this notice—and in order to keep posted in the latest and best things in stove manufacture, you must keep in constant touch with Mt. Penn. Wherever you see the word "Penn" in connection with another word making up the name of a stove, "that's us."

Torrid Sunshine Furnaces

Keep Warm

As long as you can.

As easy as you can.

As cheap as you can.

You want a furnace for the church or home. You should have the best. There is a difference in furnaces. You cannot judge by size, nor dare you depend upon all that makers tell you, but you may safely believe what users say. So please send for our furnace book, and notice the ringing testimonials from people all over the land. Some of them you will surely know.

Thousands of Torrid Sunshine Furnaces are in use, making people comfortable and happy everywhere.

We make all desirable sizes and styles, either with a steel plate radiator, all cast radiator, and for hot air and hot water combined.

Remember, every furnace is fully warranted.

We are specialists in heating and ventilation, and will take pleasure in promptly furnishing any desired information.

Learn all about the Torrid Sunshine Furnace and you will buy no other.

Sold by the best dealers everywhere. Correspondence solicited.

THE READING STOVE WORKS,

ORR, PAINTER & CO.

MAIN OFFICE:

Reading, Pa.

64-66 North Second St., Philadelphia
15-19 West Lake St., Chicago
86 Canal St., Boston
411 William St., Buffalo

THE

Manual of Receipts

BEING A COLLECTION OF

FORMULÆ AND PROCESSES FOR ARTISANS, GIVING THE COMPOSITION OF VARIOUS ALLOYS, AMALGAMS, SOLDERS, BRONZES, LACQUERS, VARNISHES, CEMENTS, ETC., ALSO DATA FOR THE PRESERVATION AND DECORATION OF VARIOUS METALLIC ARTICLES.

COMPILED

FROM THE FILES OF THE AMERICAN ARTISAN
AND VARIOUS OTHER SOURCES

BY

SIDNEY P. JOHNSTON

1899
THE AMERICAN ARTISAN PRESS
69 Dearborn Street
CHICAGO

PREFACE.

Not so very many years ago the publication of a book such as this one would have been an impossibility, as metal workers guarded their secrets with jealous care and would, under no consideration, give out the slightest inkling as to the composition of the various lacquers, alloys, etc., used in the manufacture of various articles.

The stride taken by analytical chemistry has changed all this, and recent years have seen publicity thrown on the ingredients of many components absolutely unknown before.

In the preparation of this volume I have freely availed myself of the vast store of metal receipts and processes contained in The American Artisan during the nineteen years of its existence. These aforesaid receipts and processes are certainly of special value to sheet metal workers, as they have at one time or another been asked for by readers of that paper, and in a number of cases the information given was furnished by manufacturers using the receipt in their business or by skilled mechanics furnishing a compound whose ingredients they had themselves worked out, these valuable data being first published in The American Artisan and never having appeared in book form until now.

I must also acknowledge my indebtedness in the compilation of this volume to leading American and foreign technical journals, notably those published in Germany in behalf of the metal industry, from whose columns I have from time to time clipped receipts, the cream of which is given herewith.

I would caution those attempting a practical application of these receipts to be careful that their ingredients are proportioned with exactitude, and in case of a failure on a first attempt to make a second trial, as a too large or too small proportion of some ingredient or the improper manipulation of same can generally be proven the cause of failure. Experimentation with small quantities at first is also advisable.

THE COMPILER.

Chicago, January 4, 1899.

THE

AMERICAN ARTISAN

MANUAL OF RECEIPTS.

ACETATE OF LEAD.

Acetate of lead is obtained by the dissolution of litharge in acetic acid. It is poisonous.

AGATE WARE—REPAIRING.

To mend agate ware, place the article to be repaired on a square or mandrel stake and hammer on the defective spot, when the coating will come off of a sufficient space to solder or patch.

AICH METAL.

Aich metal is a copper-zinc alloy composed of

60 parts Copper,
38 2-10 parts Zinc,
1 8-10 parts Iron.

ALLOY FOR COLD SOLDERING.

An alloy for cold soldering is made by mixing in a cast-iron mortar

20 to 30 parts finely-powdered Copper,
with
Concentrated Sulphuric Acid,

to which

70 parts Mercury

are then added. This finely powdered copper is

secured by the addition of zinc to a sulphate of copper solution.

The amalgam formed from the mixture in the mortar is thoroughly washed with water in order to bring about the removal of the sulphuric acid, and after being left alone for a little while it becomes hard enough for scratching lead. When this alloy is employed for soldering it is heated until the assumption on its part of the consistency of wax, in which condition to the joint is made.

ALLOY FOR HOLES IN CASTINGS.

Holes in castings can be filled up by pouring liquid cast-iron into the holes and removing the superfluous metal by an iron straight-edge. It is usually preferred, however, to fill up these cavities with an alloy having a similar appearance to the cast-iron, but being much more fusible. One such alloy consists of antimony 69 parts (by weight), copper 16 parts, tin 2; melted together, to which add afterwards lead 13 parts.

ALLOY FOR SOLDER.

A soft alloy which attaches itself so firmly to the surface of metals, glass and porcelain that it can be employed to solder articles that will not bear high temperature, can be made as follows: Copper dust obtained by precipitation from the solution of the sulphate by means of zinc is put in a cast-iron or porcelain-lined mortar and mixed with strong sulphuric acid, specific gravity, 1.85. From twenty to thirty-six parts of the dust are taken, according to the hardness desired. To the cake formed of acid and copper there is added, under the constant stirring, seventy parts of mercury. When well mixed the amalgam is carefuly rinsed with warm water to remove all the acid and then set aside to cool. In ten or twelve hours it is hard enough to scratch tin. If it is to be used now, it is to be heated so hot that when worked over and brayed in a mortar it becomes as soft as wax. In this ductile form it can be spread out on any surface, to which it adheres with great tenacity when it gets cold and hard.

ALLOYS—JAPANESE.

In Japan some specialties in metallic alloys are in use, whose composition is as follows: Shadke consists of copper with 1 to 10 per cent. of gold. Articles made from this alloy are laid in a pickle of blue vitriol, alum and verdigris, until they acquire a bluish-black color. Gui-shi-bu-ichi is an alloy of copper containing 30 to 50 per cent. of silver. It possesses a peculiar gray shade. Mokume consists of several compositions. Thus, about thirty gold foils (genuine) are welded together with shadke, copper, silver and gui-shi-bu-ichi, and pierced. The pierced holes are, after firm hammering together of the plates, filled up with the above named pickle. The finest Japanese brass consists of 10 parts copper and 8 parts zinc, and is called "siachu." The bell-metal, "karakane," is composed of copper, 10 parts; tin, 10 parts; iron, 0.5 part; and zinc, 1.5 parts. The copper is first fused, then the remaining metals are added in rotation.

ALLOY—LIPOWITZ'S.

Lipowitz's alloy is composed of tin (4 parts), lead (8 parts), cadmium (3 parts), bismuth (15 parts).

ALLOY—MOUSSET'S SILVER.

Mousset's silver alloy is composed of

27 56-100 parts Silver,
9 57-100 parts Zinc,
3 42-100 parts Nickel,
56 6-110 parts Copper.

It is yellow in color, with a reddish tinge.

ALLOY OF TIN AND COPPER.

An alloy of 95 parts of tin and 5 parts of copper will connect metals with glass, according to the Pharmaceutical Record. The alloy is prepared by pouring the copper into the molten tin, stirring with a wooden mixer, and afterwards remelting. It adheres strongly to clean glass surfaces and has nearly the same rate of expansion as glass. By adding from one-half to one per cent. of lead or zinc the alloy may be rendered softer or harder, or more or less easily fusible, as required. It may also be used for coating metals, imparting to them a silvery appearance.

ALLOY—WOOD'S.

Is composed of tin (2 parts), lead (4 parts), cadmium (1 to 2 parts), bismuth (5 to 8 parts).

ALUMINUM BRASS.

Aluminum brass is an alloy composed of aluminum with zinc and copper. Some of the commoner proportions of these ingredients are as follows:

(1) 67 4-10 parts Copper,
26 8-10 parts Zinc,
5 8-10 parts Aluminum.

(2) 67 parts Copper,
30 parts Zinc,
3 parts Aluminum.

(3) 71 parts Copper,
27 5-10 parts Zinc,
1 5-10 parts Aluminum.

(4) 57 parts Copper,
42 parts Zinc,
1 part Aluminum.

(5) 70 parts Copper,
27 5-10 parts Zinc,
2 5-10 parts Aluminum.

ALUMINUM COATING FOR IRON AND STEEL.

The aluminum process for the decoration and preservation of iron and steel is intended to take the place of nickeling, tinning and coppering. The coating leaves the sharpness of the outline unimpaired and adheres closely to cast and wrought iron.

AMALGAM—ARRINGTON.

Arrington amalgam is composed of the following: Silver, 40 per cent.; tin, 60 per cent.

AMALGAM—DIAMOND.

Diamond amalgam is composed of the following: Silver, 31.76; tin, 66.74; gold, 1.50.

AMALGAM—HOOD'S.

Hood's amalgam is composed of the following: Silver, 34.64; tin, 60.37; gold, 2.70; iron, 2.90.

AMALGAM—JOHNSON & LUND'S.

Johnson & Lund's amalgam is composed of the following: Silver, 38.27; tin, 59.58; platinum, 1.34; gold, 0.81.

AMALGAM—LAWRENCE'S.

Lawrence's amalgam is composed of the following: Silver, 47.87; tin, 33.68; copper, 14.91; gold, 3.54.

AMALGAM LIQUID FOR SILVERING GLOBES, ETC.

Pure lead and grain tin each 1 ounce. Melt in a clear ladle and immediately add 1 ounce bismuth. Skim off the dross, remove the ladle from the fire, and before the metal sets add 1 ounce quicksilver. Stir the compound well, aviding the fumes evolved.

AMALGAM—TOWNSEND'S.

Townsend's amalgam is composed of the following: Silver, 40.21; tin, 47.54; copper, 10.65; gold, 1.6.

AMALGAM—TOWNSEND'S IMPROVED.

Townsend's improved amalgam is composed of the following: Silver, 39.00; tin, 55.65; gold, 5.31.

AMALGAM—WALKER'S.

Silver, 34.89; tin, 60.01; platinum, 0.96; gold, 4.14.

AMMONIA FERROUS SULPHATE.

Ammonia ferrous sulphate is made by the dissolution, in an extremely small quantity of water, of

60 parts Ammonium-sulphate,
139 parts Ferrous sulphide.

The solution is heated to 140 degrees Fahrenheit, then poured into a porcelain dish, to which a few drops of sulphuric acid are added, the mass being stirred until cool. The deposition of a pale-blue crystalline meal ensues. This is dried 24 hours afterward in a funnel, the tube of which is to be closed by a tuft of cotton.

ANNEALING STEEL.

The pieces of steel to be annealed are heated very slowly, and when at a low, red heat they are placed between two dry boards and then screwed up tight in a vise. The steel burns its way into the boards, and as they come together around it an air-tight charcoal bed is formed. On this cooling the steel is found thoroughly annealed. Another method of annealing steel is to heat same to a dull red heat, cover it with dry, warm sand, and leave it to cool slowly. It may also be heated and covered up in a forge fire and left there until the fire is out.

A third method is to heat the steel red hot until evenly heated, then removing it from the fire to some dark place and let it cool until the dull red can be no longer seen in the darkness. The steel is then cooled in cold water.

ANTI-FRICTION COMPOSITION.

An anti-friction composition, used with great success in Bavaria, instead of oil, tallow, etc., is thus made: 10½ parts of lard are melted with 2 parts of pulverized plumbago; the lard is melted, the plumbago mixed in slowly, stirred well, and the mixture applied cold.

ANTIMONOID.

The welding powder named antimonoid consists of 4 parts of iron turnings, 3 parts of borax, 2 parts of borate of iron, and 1 part of water.

ANTIMONY COLORING ON BRASS.

To give the color of antimony on brass, ½ an ounce of cream of tartar is to be dissolved in 1 pound of hot water, to which is added 2 ounces pulverized metallic antimony and 2 ounces hydro-chloric acid. This fluid is to be heated to the boiling point and the brass objects plunged therein. They then acquire a lustrous color of great beauty, the first tint to appear being a gold-yellow and the second color a copper-red, the third color appearing is a blue-violet and the fourth is a blue-green. These colors will not be affected by exposure to the atmosphere.

ARGENTIC OXIDE.

Argentic oxide is precipitated as a black powder from a solution of nitrate of silver by ammonia.

ASHBERRY METAL.

Ashberry metal is an alloy made of

80 parts Tin,
14 parts Antimony,
2 parts Copper,
2 parts Nickel,
1 part Zinc,
1 part Aluminum.

It can also be made of

79 parts Tin,
15 parts Antimony,
3 parts Copper,
2 parts Zinc,
1 part Nickel.

BABBITT'S ANTI-ATTRITION METAL.

This well-known bearing metal is made by melting separately 8 parts of regulus of antimony, 12 parts of Banca tin and 4 parts of copper, and after fusing same adding 12 parts of tin. The antimony is added to the first portion of tin, and after the melting pot is taken away from the fire, and before the solution is poured into the mold, the copper is introduced. Oxidation is provided against by a surface coating of powdered charcoal. The lining metal consists of this hardening fused with twice its weight of tin, thus making it a compound 88 9-10 parts tin, 7 4-10 parts antimony and 3 7-10 parts copper. The bearing it is designed to line is cast with a shallow recess for the reception of the Babbitt metal. The part to be tinned is to be washed with alcohol and powdered with sal-ammoniac, and those surfaces which are not thus lined are covered with a clay wash. Warmth for the volatilization of a portion of the sal-ammoniac is then introduced, and the substance tinned. The lining is next cast in between a form which takes the place of the journal and the bearing.

(2) There are many compositions made and sold under the name of Babbitt metal. One of the best is copper 1 part, tin 6 parts, antimony 2 parts by weight; melt the copper in a crucible, add gradually one-half of the tin, then the antimony, and then the rest of the tin. Let the temperature gradually fall as the tin is added, and pour into bar molds of iron.

BATTERY.

For a battery for plating small articles, take a cylindrical vessel and put it into another smaller vessel made of porous porcelain; fill the inner one with diluted sulphuric acid and the space between the two with sulphate of copper, if you desire to plate an article with copper; if not, a solution of salt of gold, silver, etc., according to what you wish it to be. Put a slip of zinc in the sulphuric acid and attach a copper wire to it and the other end to the article you wish to plate and immerse that in the first solution. If you want the metal to be very thick you must put a few solid crystals of the metal in the solution; where you do not want it to come in contact, you must touch it with a little grease.

BELGIAN POLISHING POWDER.

Belgian polishing powder for polishing silver is made of 117 parts of elutriated pipe clay, 62 parts of white lead, 23 parts of white magnesia, 23 parts of jewelers' rouge and 250 parts of whiting.

BELL METAL.

A good alloy for bell metal consists of 78 per cent. copper and 22 per cent. tin. A good bell metal has a peculiarly grayish white color that is to be readily distinguished from that of either ordinary bronze or statuary bronze. It is hard, sonorous and brittle and shows a fine grained fracture. If you cool it rapidly after it has been heated red, it becomes soft, but will recover its hardness if re-heated and cooled very slowly. The larger the proportion of copper in the alloy the deeper and graver the tone of the bell, while sharper tones are caused by the addition of zinc, iron or tin to the alloy.

BENDING TIN TUBES.

The way to bend tin, brass, or copper tubes is as follows: Make the tube with a lap seam, solder it, and solder up one end. Fill the tube with melted rosin and let it get cold. With a little care it can then be bent nicely in any shape by keeping the seam on the inside of the bend. Tubes have been bent up to ¾ inch.

BIDDERY METAL.

Biddery metal is made of

84 3-10 parts Zinc,
11 4-10 parts Copper,
2 9-10 parts Lead,
1 4-10 parts Tin,
or from
93 4-10 parts Zinc,
3 1-10 parts Lead,
3 5-10 parts Copper.

BIRMINGHAM BRITANNIA METAL.

Birmingham Sheet Britannia metal is composed of

1 5-10 parts Copper,
7 8-10 parts Antimony,
90 6-10 parts Tin.

Birmingham Cast Britannia metal is composed of
9-100 parts Copper,
9 2-10 parts Antimony,
90 71-100 parts Tin.

BISMUTH NITRATE.

Bismuth nitrate is obtained by the dissolution of bismuth in nitric acid.

BLACKENING COPPER.

A good black finish to copper it given by putting same in a pickle consisting of 4 parts of concentrated hydro-chloric acid, 1 part sulphuric acid (of 66 degrees Be), and 2 parts arsenic acid and 24 of water. This pickle is to be heated before using.

BLAOKENING SHEET IRON.

The simplest method to blacken iron is to heat it with oil, especially linseed. The objects are first rubbed or painted with oil and then heated to such an extent that the oil is burned off. The surface produced in this manner is coal black, and gives the objects a black coloring, whioh will withstand the highest temperature. After the application is thoroughly dried, the objects can be rubbed with benzine or a solution of soda. In order to produce a black asphalte lac for iron, melt 8 pounds of asphalte in an iron kettle, gradually adding 12 pints of cooked linseed oil, 1 pound of litharge, and ½ pound of sulphate of zinc. The whole mixture should be allowed to boil three hours. Finally, 1½ pounds black umber is to be added, and the mixture carefully boiled for two hours longer. It is advisable previous to using this mixture to thin it by the addition of oil of turpentine.

BLACK—IRON.

Iron black is a finely divided antimony powder, which is precipitated from a solution of antimony by zinc.

BLACKING—HARNESS.

Some good receipts for harness blacking are made as follows:

1. Treacle, ½ pound; lampblack, 1 ounce; yeast, a spoonful; sugar candy, olive oil, gum tragacanth and isinglass each 1 ounce; and a cow's gall. Mix with 2 pints of stale beer and let it stand before the fire one hour.

2. Treacle, 8 parts; lampblack, 1 part; sweet oil, gum arabic, 1; isinglass, 1; water, 32. Apply heat to the whole. When cold add 1 ounce of spirits of wine and apply with a sponge. If it should get hard, place the bottle in warm water a short time.

BLACKING SHEET ZINC.

For blacking sheet zinc for the purpose of drawing lines, so that the blacking will not rub off, also answers for cast-iron, wrought-iron and steel. To 4 ounces of clear water add 1 onnce of powdered sulphate of copper, then ½ teaspoonful of nitric acid. Before applying this solution, be sure and brighten the surface which is to be coated. When using, dampen a clean part of waste, passing it over the work. When the surface is large use different parts of the dampened waste, so that the surface will have the same color. Generally the waste turns black after being drawn across the work, and also produces black streaks on the surface coats. This applies only to cast-iron, wrought-iron and steel. These metals when coated have the appearance of copper; but with zinc the surface is black. Rub the surface dry, after aplying with clean waste.

BLACKING—STOVE.

The following formula is said to make an excellent stove blacking: Two parts copperas, 1 part bone-black, 1 part black lead, mixed to consistency of cream with water. Make two applications of the polish to the stove.

(2) A quick-drying stove blacking with a good gloss is made thusly: Take 2 pounds plumbago, 5 gills

Japan dryer of furniture varnish, 1 gill asphaltum varnish and thin down for use with gasoline. Lampblack may be substituted for asphaltum if desired, a trial of which will determine the quantity. Mix only as desired for immediate use.

(3) Several valuable receipts for stove blacking are given herewith:

(1) To 1 gallon benzine add 6 ounces pulverized rosin, 3 ounces pulverized borax, 4 ounces pulverized alum, 1 pound fine ground black lead, and 1 to 2 ounces lampblack. Apply to the stove with a soft brush. For bright goods omit the blacks. (2) Reduce cheap Japan to the thickness of cream and apply to all parts of the stove with a brush, covering as much space as can be polished before it sets; then sprinkle on best quality of powdered lead, rub briskly with a hard brush and polish with a dry brush. (3) To 1 gallon gasoline or naphtha add 6 ounces pulverized resin, 1 pound pulverized lead, 3 ounces lampblack; put in a tight can and shake thoroughly; pour out in quantities for immediate use only. (4) To 1 gallon benzine add ½ pound pulverized resin, 1 pound fine ground lead, ½ ounce borax, and to give luster add 2 ounces lampblack. In mixing stove polish for sample stoves gasoline instead of benzine is recommended, as the quality is much improved by its use, and for stoves in use turpentine is recommended, as it will not give any unpleasant odor when the stove is in use.

BLUE COLOR FOR IRON AND STEEL.

To give iron and steel a bluish color cleanse the article thoroughly with lime and then brush it over with a mixture composed of the following ingredients:

16 parts Hydro-chloric Acid,
8 parts Fuming Nitric Acid,
8 parts Butter of Antimony.

Hydro-chloric acid is to be added drop by drop very slowly, in order to avoid heating. The mixture is to be applied to the steel with a cloth; the steel is then rubbed with green young oak wood until the blue color desired is produced.

BLUE PRINT PROCESS.

The process is a simple one, requiring for its manipulation to obtain best results, prepared, or heliographic paper, a copying frame, glass and cushion, which may be obtained of dealers in artists' materials. In use the frame is laid on the glass side, the back and cushion removed. The tracing or drawing (which has been made with deep black India ink upon tracing paper or cloth) is laid on the glass face downward, the prepared paper placed over it, the prepared side next to the tracing, the cushion placed over this and the back of the frame closed. Care must be used to have the tracing, the prepared paper and the cushion perfectly smooth, so as to insure the perfect contact of the tracing and paper. Reverse the frame and expose to the light for from six minutes to an hour, according to the degree of light. Remove the prepared paper and drench in clear water ten minutes or more, and hang by one edge to dry. The prepared paper requires to be entirely shielded from daylight before being used and while putting it into the frame. Where all the regular materials are not at hand the cushion may be a smoothly-folded blanket placed upon a board, and on this laid successively the prepared paper, the tracing and the plate glass.

BLUE PRINTS.

The following two formulas for making blue prints are in general use. They both make good prints, but the one marked No. 2 gives the clearer print.

No. 1—

1 oz. of Red Potash,
1 oz. of Citrate Iron of Ammonium,
1 pint of Water.

No. 2—

1 oz. of Red Potash,
1¼ oz. of Citrate Iron of Ammonium,
1½ pints of Water.

BLUING SHEET-STEEL.

To give small articles of sheet-steel a blue appearance dip them in a fluid alloy consisting of 25 parts of lead and 1 part of tin, melted at the requisite degree of heat for bluing. This dipping may also be made in a sand bath and maintained at the requisite temperature, of 4.78 degrees Fahrenheit for the pale blue and 5.72 degrees Fahrenheit for dark blue.

BLUING STEEL.

Steel is "blued" by heating it evenly in an ash bath —that is, a quantity of sand is spread over a sheet of boiler iron and heated up to about the boiling point of oil, say 600 degrees. If a little oil is rubbed over the surfaces with a piece of waste the color will be better. All articles to be colored should be polished.

BLUING STEEL OR IRON.

To put a durable blue on iron or steel without heat, apply nitric acid and let it eat into the iron a little, then the metal will be covered with a fine film of oxide. Clean, oil and varnish.

BRASS—ANTIQUE.

To produce the appearance of antique brass, dissolve 1 ounce sal-ammoniac, 3 ounces cream of tartar, and 6 ounces common salt in 1 pint hot water; then add 2 ounces nitrate of copper dissolved in a half pint of water; mix well, and apply it repeatedly to the article by means of a brush.

BRASS—BRISTOL.

Bristol brass is composed of either

75 5-10 parts Copper,
24 5-10 parts Zinc,

or

67 2-10 parts Copper,
32 8-10 parts Zinc,

or

60 8-10 parts Copper,
39 2-10 parts Zinc.

BRASSES FOR SIDE-RODS.

Brasses for side rods are made of
1 part Tin,
6 parts Copper,
and to 100 pounds of this mixture add one-half part each of zinc and lead.

BRASS PIPE FINISH.

Take very finest flour of emery paper and oil, bringing the surface to a very smooth and even finish first. Rub well with rotten stone and oil on a piece of soft leather and finish with dry whiting and a rag. Then, if desired to lacquer, see that every part is free from oil and very clean. Take shellac varnish, thin with 95 per cent. alcohol, and let it stand a few hours to settle. Afterward apply the lacquer with a camel's hair brush, keeping the surface of the brass work very warm all the time.

BRASS—RED.

Red brass is composed of
17 parts Tin,
81 parts Copper,
2 parts Cupro-manganese,
or from
14 parts Tin,
85 parts Copper,
1 part Cupro-manganese.

BRASS—TEST FOR.

To discover the presence of lead in brass add a few drops of sulphuric acid to a solution of the brass in nitric acid. The volume of the resultant precipitation will determine the quantity of lead. If there is a large quantity of lead in the brass it becomes brittle.

BRIGHTENING TINWARE.

To brighten up shop-worm tin ware and make it look like new, dip a soft cloth in plaster-of-paris and rub the ware. Putz pomade is too expensive and too much trouble to get off. Almost all the other polishes contain more or less acid.

BRILLIANT BLACK FOR IRON AND STEEL.

To produce a brilliant black upon iron and steel, apply with a fine hair brush a mixture of turpentine and sulphur which has been boiled together.

BRITANNIA METAL.

English Britannia metal is composed of

16 24-100 parts Antimony,
1 84-100 parts Copper,
81 9-10 parts Tin.
14 6-100 parts Copper,
7 81-100 parts Antimony,
90 62-100 parts Tin.
3 1-10 parts Copper,
5-10 part Zinc,
6 3-10 parts Antimony,
90 1-10 parts Tin.
3 6-100 parts Zinc,
8 1-100 parts Copper,
9 66-100 parts Antimony,
85 4-10 parts Tin.

BRONZE—ANCIENT.

Copper 100 parts, tin 7 parts, lead 7 parts.

BRONZE—BROWN FIRE-PROOF, ON COPPER AND BRASS.

A brown fire-proof bronze for copper or brass is obtained by the dissolution of 1 1-12 drachms each of finely powdered sal-ammoniac and verdigris in one pint of water, the solution being allowed to stand covered 3 to 4 hours, at which time 1½ additional pints of water are added. When bronzing a copper article, which must first be cleaned perfectly, it is to be held over a coal fire and heated to a uniform heat and color. Then cast the application of the solution, followed by careful drying. Tin copper is not to be heated sufficiently to melt the tin. Five or six such treatments of copper gives it a brass color, and from six to ten applications gives it a beautiful yellow tint. If a color shading from yellow into brown is desired for your article it must not be hot when the mixture is applied. This operation is to be repeated twenty to twenty-five times in order to give a light brown color.

BRONZE—CHEAP.

A good, cheap bronze for use on the common kind of tea-trays is made by making into a paste with oil, and melting together 4 ounces borax, 4 ounces saltpeter, 2 drachms corrosive sublimate, 8 ounces flowers of zinc and 16 ounces of verdigris.

BRONZE—COPPER.

A copper bronze is secured by coating the metal (either iron or zinc) with a brown varnish or lacquer and dusting copper-dust upon it.

BRONZE FOR CASTINGS.

A good and permanent bronze can be made by melting together 96 parts copper and 4 parts tin. The following is a good bronzing liquid: Sal-ammoniac 1 drachm, oxalic acid 15 grains, vinegar 1 pint; mix. After well cleaning the article to be bronzed, warm it gently and brush it over with the liquid, using only a small quantity at a time. When rubbed dry repeat the application until the desired tint is obtained.

BRONZE FOR CAST IRON.

To bronze cast iron, mix equal parts of petroleum oil and French yellow, to the consistency of paint, and apply hot.

BRONZE FOR GILDING.

A good bronze for gilding must be fusible at a low temperature and must also be compact and close grained. A good alloy being copper, 82 25-100 parts; zinc, 17 5-10 parts, and tin, 25-100 parts.

(2) Copper, 14 parts; zinc, 6 parts; tin, 4 parts.

BRONZE FOR GUN BARRELS.

A good receipt for bronzing gun barrels is: Aqua fortis and sweet spirits of nitre each half an ounce; sulphate of copper, 2 ounces; water, 30 ounces; tincture of muriate of iron, 1 ounce. Mix and apply.

BRONZE FOR IRON OR BRASS.

Articles of iron or brass may be bronzed by dipping them into melted sulphur mixed with lampblack. The surface, after being drained off, will take a beautiful polish, and presents the appearance of oxidized bronze.

BRONZE FOR MEDALS, SMALL CASTINGS, ETC.

Copper, 95 parts; tin, 4 parts. Melt together.

BRONZE FOR SMALL CASTINGS.

A fine bronze for small castings is composed of 94 12-100 parts of copper and 5 88-100 parts tin.

BRONZE—GOLD.

A very handsome gold bronze alloy is made of 90 5-10 parts copper, 6 5-10 parts tin, 3 parts zinc. This alloy should not be exposed to water, as it will then lose its gold color.

BRONZE—GREEN FOR BRASS.

A green bronze for brass is obtained by mixing 1 part of green vitriol, 1 part of gum arabic, 1 part of sal-ammoniac, 1 part of red umber, 1 part of mineral green, 80 parts of strong vinegar and 4 parts of Avignon berries. Cleanse the articles to be bronzed with diluted nitric acid, then rinse them with water and apply the fluid with a brush. If the color is not then satisfactorily dark the article is to be heated until too warm to be held in the hand, and then given a coat of spirit of wine mixed with a little lampblack. Finish the work by applying a coat of spirit of varnish Another green bronze for brass is obtained by adding to a solution of 8 drachms of copper in 1 ounce of strong nitric acid, 3½ drachms sal-ammoniac, 6¾ drachms aqua-ammonia and 10½ ounces vinegar. This liquid is to be placed in a bottle not tightly corked, and allowed to stand in a warm place for several days. After it has been applied to any object it should be dried by exposure to heat, and when dry a coat of linseed oil varnish should be applied, which is also dried by heat.

BRONZE—GREEN FOR TIN.

A green bronze for tin, zinc and lead can be secured by applying lacquer of a dull luster, or green varnish. The best green for bronze is made by a mixture of chrome yellow with Frankfort black.

BRONZE—LIQUID.

An admirable bronze liquid is made by the dissolution of ½ ounce of alum, ¼ ounce of arsenic and 1 ounce of sal-ammoniac in 1 pint of strong vinegar.

BRONZE—METAL.

Copper, 27½ parts; zinc, 12 parts; tin, 8 parts. Melt together.

BRONZE—ORMOLU.

The composition of ormolu bronze is 58 3-10 parts copper, 25 3-10 parts zinc and 16 7-10 parts tin.

BRONZE—PATINA ON TIN.

A bronze patina on tin is obtained by brushing the article with a solution of 1¾ ounces sulphate of copper, 1¾ ounces ferrous sulphate in 1 quart of water, then wetting the dried object with a solution of 3½ ounces of verdigris in 10½ ounces of vinegar. After drying, the object is to be polished with a soft brush rubbed upon wax and some iron rust. This coating should be protected by lacquer.

BRONZE—PERUVIAN.

The bronzes that Pizarro found in Peru, and which excited the admiration of Europe when introduced, were composed of 95 parts copper, 4 5-10 parts tin, 3-10 parts iron and 2-10 parts lead.

BRONZE—PHOSPHOR.

This substance, which is largely used in place of bronze and gun metal compositions, for bearings, wire, rope, gearing, etc., is a copper-tin alloy, fluxed by the introduction of a quantity of phosphor. The addition of this latter is generally made in the form of phosphide and tin or phosphide and copper.

BRONZE—STATUARY.

The bronze for use in statuary must become thinly fluid. It must also acquire a beautiful green color, technically known as patina, on brief exposure to the atmosphere. As practically the sole use of this bronze is for artistic purposes, the color is very important. The bronze at present most in vogue for statuary consists of 86 6-10 per cent. of copper, 6 6-10 per cent. tin, 3 3-10 per cent. lead and 3 3-10 per cent. zinc.

BRONZE—SUN.

Sun bronze is an alloy composed of 60 parts cobalt or 40 parts cobalt, 10 parts aluminum, 40 or 30 parts copper.

BRONZE—TUCKER.

To obtain Tucker bronze, grease polished iron and expose it for from two to five minutes to the action of vapors arising from a bath of equal parts of concentrated hydro-chlorate and nitric acid. Next coat the iron with vaseline and heat until the decomposition of the latter (or vaseline) commences.

BRONZING BRASS ARTICLES.

To bronze small brass articles, clean same well to get rid of grease, etc., and apply, with a brush, a mixture consisting of

3 parts Oxide of Iron,
3 parts White Arsenic,
36 parts Hydro-chloric Acid.

The process is finished by oiling well, after which the article may be lacquered or varnished.

BRONZING CAST-IRON.

To bronze cast-iron the first step is to clean the surface and then coat it uniformly with a layer of olive oil (a low grade will answer), then heat it without, however, raising the temperature to the burning point of the oil. This will cause the cast-iron, at the minute the decomposition of the oil is accomplished, to absorb oxygen and will cause the formation of a brown surface of oxide, whose adherence is very firm. It will acquire a good polish, thus giving the surface of the cast-iron a bronze-like appearance.

BRONZING COPPER.

A good bronze for copper is made by the dissolution of

30 parts Hydro-chlorate Ammonium,
10 parts Cream of Tartar,
10 parts Common Salt,
10 parts Acetate of Copper,
100 parts Acetate Acid,

moderately concentrated or in 200 parts of strong vinegar; a little water is to be added to this. When the mixture has become homogeneous the copper object is daubed with it and allowed to dry at an ordinary temperature at from 24 to 48 hours. When this period of time has elapsed the copper object will be found covered with verdigris, presenting a variety of tints. The whole, especially the reliefs, are to be brushed with a wax brush, and if necessary the high reliefs should be set off with chrome yellow or hematite. If you wish to deepen the color of the parts on which the bronzing is, lead carbonate of ammonia may be used. Light touches of ammonia will give a bluish tint to the green portions. If you wish to give the copper a bluish-green bronze, apply to its surface a fluid obtained by warm digestion of cinnabar with a solution of sodium sulphide, to which an addition of caustic lime has been made.

BRONZING COPPER AND BRASS.

To bronze copper and brass neutralize 20 parts of ammonia with vinegar and compound the solution with 6 parts sal-ammoniac and 10 parts verdigris. First rid your object of grease, then brush with the solution, the operation being repeated until the shade of color wanted is produced. After this has been secured pour off the solution and recleanse by hot water. Repeat the rinsing twice. The best drier for articles is sawdust.

BRONZING—GREEN.

A fine antique green bronze is obtained by repeated alternate applications to brass or copper of diluted acetic acid and exposure to the fumes of ammonia. A more rapid method for giving this appearance is found in the immersion of the articles in a solution of 1 part of per-chloride of iron in 2 parts of water. The longer the immersion the darker the shade. A second method consists in boiling the articles in a strong solution of nitrate of copper. A third method is the immersion of 2 ounces of hypo-sulphate of sodium and 2 ounces of nitrate of iron in 1 pint of water.

BRONZING IRON.

Iron articles are easily coppered or brassed by dipping in copper solutions, or else coppered or brassed by the galvanic method; these coatings also scale off after a short time, especially if the iron surface was not thoroughly cleaned, when exposed to the influence of moist air. By the following process it is easy to provide iron articles with a handsome bronze-colored protoxide coating; it resists the influence of humidity pretty well, and besides this, the operator has it in his power to produce any desired bronze color in a simple manner.

The cleansed and scoured articles are exposed to the vapors of a heated mixture of concentrated hydrochloric and nitric acids (1 and 1) for from two to five minutes; and then, without unnecessarily touching them, heated to a temperature of 300 to 350 degrees. The heating is continued until the bronze color becomes visible upon the articles. After they have been cooled, they are tubbed over with petroleum jelly, and again heated until the jelly begins to decompose. After cooling, the article is anew rubbed over with petroleum jelly. If now the vapors from a mixture of concentrated hydrochloric and nitric acids are permitted to operate upon the iron article, light red-brown tones are obtained. However, if acetic acid is mixed to the mentioned two acids, and the vapors permitted to operate upon the iron, oxide coatings are obtained, possessing a handsome bronze yellow color. All graduations of color from dark red-brown to light red-brown or from bronze-yellow to dark brown-yellow are produced by varying the mixtures of the acids.

(2) Iron has sometimes to be bronzed for domestic use. The following is a very simple way of obtaining a good bronze: Mix an equal quantity of butter of antimony and oil of olives; put this mixture on the iron which is required to be bronzed with a brush, the iron having been previously brightened with emery and cloth, and leave it for several hours. Then rub with wax and varnish with copal.

BRONZING IRON OR STEEL.

To secure a bronze-like surface on iron and steel, and one impervious to oxidation, first clean the object, then expose for two or three minutes to the action of the fumes of a heated mixture of nitric and hydro-chlorate acid in equal proportions at a temperature ranging from 550 degrees to 660 degrees Fahrenheit. When the object has cooled rub it with vaseline and then heat until decomposition of the vaseline commences. Repeat the vaseline treatment. Should a coloring lighter than bronze be desired, mix acetic acid with the other acids. In making this bronze one should be very careful both in handling and preserving these acids.

BRONZING MEDALS.

First clean the medal, then apply on its surface a thin paste made of water with equal parts of peroxide of iron and plumbago, with a small proportion of clay. Heat the whole, and when the object has cooled, brush vigorously for a long time with a medium stiff brush, which is frequently rubbed upon a yellow waxen black and afterwards upon the mixture of peroxide of iron and plumbago.

BRONZING TIN.

To bronze tin, prepare two solutions.

(1) 1 part of Ferrous Sulphate,
1 part of Cupric Sulphate,
20 parts of Distilled Water,

(2) 4 parts Verdigris,
16 parts Vinegar.

The article to be bronzed is to be thoroughly cleansed by means of a brush dipped in a fine earth and water, and after it is dry a light coat of the first solution is to be applied to both sides by means of a brush. When it is dry the article looks black; then the second solution is to be applied with a brush until the article assumes a dark copper-red color. Then allow it to dry for one hour, and polish with a soft brush and finely powdered elutriated blood-stone, the surface being often breathed upon in order to secure adhesion of the blood-stone. Then polish it with the brush which is from time to time drawn over the palm of the hand. The bronzing is protected against dampness by covering with a very thin layer of gold lacquer.

(2) Tin and tin alloys, after careful cleansing from oxide and grease, are handsomely and permanently bronzed if brushed over with a solution of 1 part of sulphate of copper (blue-stone), and 1 part of sulphate of iron (copperas) in 20 parts of water. When this has dried, the surface should be brushed with a solution of one part of acetate of copper (verdigris) in acetic acid.

After several applications and dryings of the last named, the surface is polished with a soft brush and blood-stone powder. The raised portions are then rubbed off with soft leather moistened with wax and turpentine, followed by a rubbing with dry leather.

BRONZING ZINC.

Zinc, which is to be bronzed, should be given an electro-deposition of brass, which is then dipped into a weak solution of sulphate of copper in order to impart a red tint. When it is dry, moisten with a cloth immersed in hydro-sulphate of ammonia or proto-chloride of copper dissolved in hydro-chloric acid, or a solution of polysulphide of potassium. Dry again, then brush the surface over with a mixture of peroxide of iron and plumbago, varied in accordance with the tint desired. The powder will adhere more readily if the brush is slightly moistened with essence of turpentine. Rub the raised portions strongly to uncover the brass, then give a coat of colorless varnish. Another way is to pickle the brass or copper article with diluted nitric acid, then coat same with a paste made of 2 parts graphite, 3 parts peroxide of iron and enough spirits of wine. Brush off this coating after 24 hours, and a dark-brown bronze will appear. If a lighter bronze is desired, the brass or copper zinc should be rubbed with a soft brush dipped in a solution of 1¼ ounces of sal-ammoniac and 3 ounces of potassium binoxalate in 3½ to 5¼ pints of vinegar.

BROWNING COPPER.

To give copper a brown color scour it bright with glass paper, heat over a coal fire and then brush over with a solution consisting of

3 parts Diluted Acetic Acid,
7 parts Sal-ammoniac,
5 parts Crystallized Acetate of Copper,
85 parts Distilled Water,

and then rub the article with a solution consisting of

4 parts Oil of Turpentine,
1 part Wax.

BROWNING COPPER—LIQUID FOR.

A liquid for giving a brown tinge to copper is made by the addition to acetic acid of 11 drachms of spirit of sal-ammoniac; blue litmus paper, when dipped in same, becomes red. Next add 5½ drachms of sal-ammoniac and enough water to make 2 pints. This fluid is to be used, wetting the copper surface again and again, and rubbing after each application until the brown tint desired is obtained.

BROWNING METAL.

A good brown on metal may be had by dissolving 68 grams of carbonate of ammonia in 1,000 grams of hot water, to which 56 grams of citrate of copper oxide should be added while stirring, and then 100 grams of verdigris and 25 grams of alum that has been previously dissolved in 200 grams of water should be added, and finally 10 grams of oxalic acid. Brush twice with tartar water.

BRUNSWICK BLACK.

Brunswick black is made as follows:

(1) Foreign asphaltum, 45 pounds; drying oil, 6 gallons; litharge, 6 pounds. Boil and thin with 25 gallons of oil or turpentine. Used for iron work, etc.

(2) Black pitch and gas tar asphaltum, of each 25 pounds; boil gently for five hours; then add linseed oil, 8 gallons; litharge and red lead, of each, 10 pounds; boil slowly, and thin with oil of turpentine, 20 gallons. Inferior to the other, but cheaper.

BURNISHING SILVER.

The first step in burnishing silver is to clean off any dirt which the surfaces of the silver articles may have contracted during the process of their manufacture. To do this take pumice-stone powder and with a brush saturated in strong soapsuds rub the various parts of the article, even those which are to remain a dull color, which, nevertheless, are thus given a beautiful white appearance. After wiping with an old linen rag go ahead with the burnishing.

BURNT CAST-STEEL—TO RESTORE.

To restore burnt cast-steel use a mixture consisting of

1 part Dragons' Blood,
8 parts Salt-petre,
4 parts Colophony.

The article is to be heated to a dark-red heat and dusted with this compound. After the absorption of the powder is complete the article is to be thoroughly worked upon an anvil.

(2) Another compound for this purpose consists of

4 parts Salt-petre,
½ part Gum Arabic,
½ part Aloes,
¼ part Resin,
8 parts Red Chromate of Potassium,

with which the steel, when red-hot, is dusted.

(3) Another method consists in the repeated immersion of the red-hot burnt steel in a compound of

2 parts Boiled Linseed Oil,
3 parts Colophony.

BURNT STEEL TOOLS—TO RESTORE.

To restore burnst steel tools, melt together 4 ounces of black pitch and 1 pound tallow, and then add, with constant stirring, 4 ounces of yellow prussiate of potash, 12 drachms of soap, a handful of common salt and 13 ounces of sal-ammoniac. Immerse the articles, heated red-hot, in this compound; allow them to cool and then harden them again, as customary.

(2) Another compound consists of

5 parts Fish Oil,
2 parts Tallow,
10 parts Resin,
¼ part Asafoetida.

BUTTER OF ANTIMONY.

Butter of antimony is made by heating a tri-sulphide with mercuric chloride.

CASE-HARDENING CAST-IRON.

For case-hardening cast-iron, take salt, 21 pounds; saltpetre, ½ pound; rock alum, ⅛ pound; ammonia, 4 ounces; salt of tartar, 4 ounces; pulverize all together and incorporate thoroughly. Use by powdering all over the iron while hot, then plunging in cold water.

CASE-HARDENING COMPOUND FOR IRON.

A good case-hardening for iron consists of
18 parts Sal-soda,
4 parts Muriate of Soda,
1 part Black Oxide of Manganese,
16 parts Lampblack.

CASTING IRON WITH PURE LEAD.

For casting iron or steel plates with nearly pure lead, the material to be treated is subjected to a series of five baths. The first is in a pickle, through which a weak current of electricity is passed. This bath removes the scales from the surface of the metal, and the electricity is said to greatly expedite matters. The second bath is in lime water, which neutralizes the acid. Then comes the bath in clear water. The fourth bath is in a neutral solution of zinc and stannic chlorides. The drying process, which follows, leaves on the surface of the plates a deposit of the mixed metallic chlorides, which protects the plates from oxidation. The next process consists in passing the plates through a bath of molten deal, and when taken from here the metal is found to be coated with an adherent layer of lead, which, though thin, is uniformly spread. It is said this process has no decreasing effect on the ductility or strength of the iron, and that a plate may be bent, closed and opened again without cracking the coating.

CEMENT—ACID PROOF.

(1) To make an acid proof cement mix oxide of zinc with a concentrated solution of zinc chloride.

(2) A cement capable of resisting the action of

acidulous fumes is composed of a concentrated solution of silicate of soda formed into paste with powdered glass.

CEMENT—AQUARIUM.

Cement for aquariums can be prepared in the following way:

(1) Take 1 gill of litharge, 1 gill of plaster of paris, 1 gill of fine white sand, 1-3 of a gill of finely powdered resin. Mix well and bottle and cork it until it is wanted for use; then mix it with boiled linseed oil and dryers until as thick as putty. Mix the cement only in small quantities, as it dries quickly.

(2) Mix boiled linseed oil, litharge, red and white lead together, using white lead in the largest proportion; spread on flannel and place in the joints.

(3) A solution of glue, 8 ounces, to 1 ounce of Venice turpentine; boil together, agitating all the time, until the mixture becomes as complete as possible, the joints to be cemented to be kept together for forty-eight hours if required.

(4) Take half a gill of gold size, 2 gills of red lead, 1½ gills of litharge, and sufficient silver-sand to make into a thick paste for use. This mixture sets in about two days.

(5) Mix well-dried Venetian red, 3 pounds, with oxide of iron, 1 pound, and add as much boiled oil as will make the mixture into a stiff paste.

(6) Common putty and litharge in about equal quantities, well mixed with boiled linseed oil.

CEMENT—BLACK IRON FOR IRON OVENS.

Black iron cement for iron ovens is composed of the following: Iron filings (10 parts), sand (12 parts), bone black (10 parts), slaked lime (12 parts), lime milk (5 parts).

CEMENT—BOTTLE CORK.

The bituminous or black cement for bottle corks consists of pitch hardened by the addition of rosin and brick dust.

CEMENT—DIAMOND.

The so-called Diamond cement for use in steam apparatus, steam boilers, etc., is made of 50 parts prepared graphite, 16 parts litharge, 15 parts whiting and 16 parts of linseed oil varnish.

CEMENT—ELECTRICAL.

A cement for use in fixing electrical or chemical apparatus is prepared by the mixture of 2 ounces plaster of paris, 1 pound of wax, 1 pound of red ochre, 5 pounds of rosin; the entire mass being melted at a moderate heat.

CEMENT—EVANS' METALLIC.

Evan's Metallic Cement is made by the dissolution of a cadmium amalgam prepared from 25 99-100 parts cadmium and 74 1-100 parts mercury in an excess of mercury, the solution being slightly packed in a leather bag and intimately kneaded. This kneading, particularly in cases where the cement has been previously heated to about 97 degrees Fahrenheit, makes the same very plastic and similar to softened wax.

CEMENT—FIRE-PROOF.

Fire-proof cement is made as follows: To 4 or 5 parts of clay, thoroughly dried and pulverized, add 2 parts of iron filings free from oxide, 1 part of peroxide of manganese, ½ of sea salt and ½ of borax. Mix these ingredients thoroughly and render them as fine as possible, then reduce them to a thick paste with the necessary quantity of water, mixing intimately. It must be used immediately. After application it should be exposed to the heat, gradually increasing to almost a white heat. This cement is very hard.

(2) To equal parts of sifted peroxide of manganese and pulverized zinc white add a sufficient quantity of commercial soluble to form a thin paste. This mixture, when used, immediately forms a cement quite equal in hardness to that obtained by the first method.

(3) Take equal parts pulverized zinc white and

sifted peroxide of manganese, and make into a paste with soluble glass.

CEMENT—FIRE AND WATER PROOF.

(4) A fire and water proof cement is made by stirring intimately together 2 parts iron filings free from oxide, 5 parts of clay thoroughly dried and pulverized, ½ part borax, ½ part salt, 1 part of peroxide of manganese. These are made as fine as possible by stirring and then reduced to a thick paste. This cement must be used as soon as it is made. After it has been applied, it should be exposed to a gradually increasing heat that rises almost to a white heat.

Another fire and water proof cement is made by the addition of enough soluble glass to equal parts of pulverized zinc-white and sifted peroxide of manganese to form a thin paste. This cement must also be used as soon as it is made.

(5) Cement which resists heat and water is composed of the following: Lime, 10 parts; iron filings, 5 parts; vinegar, 2 parts; water, 3 parts.

CEMENT FOR AIR-TIGHT OVEN DOOR.

A cement for air-tight oven door, which must be used as soon as made, is composed by homogeneously combining 120 parts of iron filings, 1 of flowers of sulphur, 8 of powdered feldspar and 2 of pulverized sal-ammoniac made into a paste by the addition of water.

CEMENT FOR ASBESTOS.

To make a good cement or paste for pasting asbestos to tin hot-air furnace pipes. Take 2 parts litharge, 1 part dry slacked lime, and 1 part fine, dry sand. Combine them thoroughly, and add enough hot linseed oil to form a paste-like mass. It sets hard and quickly, and must be freshly prepared every time it is required for application, which application must be made only when the cement is hot.

CEMENT FOR BLAST PIPES, ETC.

A cement for use in blast pipes, hot-blast stoves, blow engines, etc., is composed of clay, 1 part; common salt, 1 part; iron filings, 15 parts. Mix with equal parts of vinegar and water.

CEMENT FOR BRASS AND GLASS.

Cement for brass and glass is made thusly: One part of wax and 5 parts of resin are melted, and into this mass are stirred ¼ part of plaster of paris and 1 part burnt ochre.

(2) Melt together 1 part of wax, 4 parts of resin—preferably pine resin—and stir into the melted mass 1 part of elutriated chalk or brick dust. Both these cements are to be applied warm to heated surfaces.

(3) For cementing brass on glass, knead a quantity of plaster of paris into twice the same quantity of resin soap, which is made by boiling 3 parts of resin and one part of caustic soda in 5 of water. This cement is used to a large extent for fastening brass tops on glass lamps. This is very strong, is unaffected by petroleum, bears heat excellently and becomes hard in from ½ to ¾ of an hour. It will harden more slowly when slaked lime, white lead or zinc-white is used in place of the plaster of paris.

CEMENT FOR CARD AND TIN.

A cement to unite card to tin is made as follows: Boil 1 ounce of borax and 2 ounces of powdered shellac in 15 ounces of water until the shellac is entirely dissolved.

CEMENT FOR CASINGS.

A good cement for filling faults in casings is made as follows: Iron filings free from rust, 10 parts; sulphur, ½; sal-ammoniac, 0.8; these are mixed with water to a thick paste, which is rammed into the "faults." This becomes strong when the iron filings are rusted. The parts which have to be cemented are treated before the operation with liquid ammonia, so as to be perfectly free from grease.

CEMENT FOR CAST-IRON TANKS.

The following cement is recommended for repairing damaged places in cast-iron tanks, cisterns, etc.: Five parts brimstone, 2 parts black lead, and 2 parts of cast-iron filings, previously sifted. Melt together, taking care that the brimstone does not catch fire. The damaged place, perfectly dry, is well heated by laying a piece of red-hot iron upon it, and is then stopped with the cement previously heated in a melting ladle until it becomes soft.

CEMENT FOR COPPER AND BRASS PIPE PARTS.

A cement for copper and brass parts of steam pipes is composed of

10 parts Copper or Brass shavings (respectively),
1 part Sulphur.
1 part Gutta-percha.
2 parts Caoutchouc.

CEMENT FOR DEFECTIVE PLACES IN CASTINGS.

In order to repair a defect in a casting, heat the defective place, lay a piece of cement upon it, pressing same down with a hot iron. The following paste will be found valuable for this purpose: One part rosin, 1 part black pitch, melted in a crucible, and enough fine iron filings added for the formation of a stiff mass.

CEMENT FOR FASTENING HOOKS IN STONE.

A cement for fastening hooks, clamps, iron rods, etc., in stone is made as follows: Make a paste of 1 part of iron filings, 3 parts of plaster of paris and glue water.

Another receipt gives 7 parts of plaster of paris to 1 of the iron filings. If it is desired that the article cemented is to stay white, iron filings should not be used and the cement should rather be made of 3 parts of white of egg, 7 parts of plaster of paris, with a large enough amount of water.

CEMENT FOR FASTENING IRON TO STONE.

To make cement for fastening iron to stone, take fine iron filings, 10 parts; plaster of paris, 30 parts; sal-ammoniac, ½. Mix to a fluid paste with weak vinegar and use at once.

CEMENT FOR FASTENING LABELS ON POLISHED NICKEL.

To fasten labels on polished nickel dissolve 400 parts by weight of coarsely powdered dextrine in 600 of water; add 20 parts glycerine and 10 of glucose and heat the mixture to 194 degrees Fahrenheit.

CEMENT FOR FASTENING METALS ON WOOD.

Mix into a thick solution of glue, finely ground chalk, until the mass gets the consistency desired.

CEMENT FOR FASTENING COPPER TO SANDSTONE.

The following compound will be found useful for fastening copper to sand-stone: Mix intimately so as to form a plastic mass 4 parts of powdered glass, 6 parts of bole, 6 parts of litharge, 4 parts of linseed-oil varnish and 7 parts of white lead. It will also fasten a number of other metals to a number of other species of stone.

CEMENT FOR GLASS.

To make a cement that will cement glass take about equal quantities of common putty and litharge, well mixed with boiled linseed oil.

CEMENT FOR GLASS PARTS ON LAMPS.

A bismuth cement for cementing the glass parts on petroleum lamps is composed of

2 parts Tin,
3 parts Lead,
2 5-10 parts Bismuth.

CEMENT FOR GLASS, WOOD AND METAL.

Concentrated sirupous glycerine mixed with finely ground litharge to a thick viscid paste makes a cement to resist heat, water, oil and acids. Glass, metal and wood may be cemented with it.

CEMENT FOR HEATED OBJECTS.

Cement for objects which have to be heated may be made as follows: Iron filings, 100 parts; clay, 50; common salt, 10; quartz sand, 20.

CEMENT FOR IRON CISTERNS.

A good cement for iron cisterns is made as follows: Finest iron filings are mixed with vinegar into a paste, which is left to stand until it becomes brown; the mass is then pressed into the joints.

CEMENT FOR IRON RAILINGS.

Here is a cement for iron railings, gratings to stoves, etc., which, it is claimed, will withstand the blows of a sledge hammer: Mix thoroughly equal parts of sulphur and white-lead with about one-sixth proportion of borax. In applying, wet the mixture with strong sulphuric acid and place a thin layer between the two pieces of iron and press firmly together. In five days it will be dry and solid like welding.

CEMENT FOR JOINTS.

A cement for filling in joints and uniting iron surfaces is made as follows: Take 100 parts iron filings, no larger than rape seed and free from rust, ½ part of flowers of sulphur and ¾ part of coarsely powdered sal-ammoniac. Wet the mixture with equal parts of vinegar and water and beat it, with a repetition of wetting until it becomes heated, brittle and dry. In this condition place it in the joints and pack in as tightly as you can with chisel and hammer, thus again making it moist and soft. Finally the joints are filled up evenly and permitted to become dry for 48 hours, after which time, if the work is well done, separate black drops will come out upon the hardened crust. For the preservation of this cement ram it into an iron pot and pour water over it. When you wish to employ it, pour off water and add to the mass taken out a large enough quantity of iron filings to give the requisite consistency and pour the water into the pot again.

(2) Another cement is composed of 1 part sal-ammoniac, 1 part sulphur, 30 parts iron fillings.

(3) Another cement is composed of pulverized cast-iron turnings, 50 parts; flowers of sulphur, 1 part; sal-ammoniac, 2 parts.

(4) Another cement is composed of pulverized iron filings 100 parts and pulverized sal-ammoniac 2 parts. Keep this compound in well-closed boxes in a dry place. For use, wet with equal parts of vinegar and water. Heat the cemented places only when they are wholly dry.

CEMENT FOR KEROSENE LAMPS.

For a cement to mend kerosene lamps, or secure them to the standard when they have become loose: Resin, 3 parts; caustic soda, 1 part; water, 5 parts, mixed with half its weight of plaster of paris. This cement sets firmly in about three-quarters of an hour and has great adhesive power. It is not permeable to kerosene, and is a low conductor of heat. Hot water attacks it but superficially.

CEMENT FOR LABELS ON NICKEL.

(1) To fasten labels on polished nickel, dissolve 400 parts by weight of coarsely powdered dextrin in 600 parts of water. To this add 10 parts of glucose and 20 parts of glycerine, and heat these ingredients to 194 degrees Fahrenheit.

(2) Dissolve 400 parts by weight of dextrin in water, this fluid to be further diluted by the addition of 200 parts by weight of water. Then add 20 parts of aluminum sulphate and 20 parts of glucose, heating the compound in a steam bath to 194 degrees Fahrenheit. At this, the mass which is at first thick,

becomes clear and thinly fluid. The first of these cements is probably the best.

CEMENT FOR LEATHER AND IRON.

For a cement for leather and iron, first paint the iron with either white or red lead. After this coating dries, cover it with a cement made of the best glue softened by soaking in cold water, and then dissolve in moderately warm vinegar, to which is added one-third of its volume of white oil of turpentine, and after it is intimately stirred in, it is applied while warm with a brush and the leather is pressed upon it.

(2) Digest 1 part of crushed nut galls for six hours with 8 parts of distilled water. Carefully strain the mass; then make a dissolution of glue soaked in its own weight of water for 24 hours. The infusion of galls is warmed and spread on the leather while the glue solution is put on the roughened surface of the heated metal. The dampened leather is pressed upon it, and when dry its adherence is so firm that its removal is impossible without tearing.

CEMENT FOR LEAK IN LEAD PIPE.

For a leak in lead pipe for hot water take a solder made of 2 parts tin to one of lead, and use with a mixture of resin and sweet oil as a flux.

CEMENT FOR LEAKY BOILERS.

A cement for leaky boilers (steam or hot water) consists of 2 parts of powdered litharge, 2 parts of fine sand, and 1 part of slacked lime. Mix with linseed oil and apply quickly.

CEMENT FOR LUTING CRUCIBLE LIDS.

For luting crucible lids apply to a concentrated solution of borax a thick paste made from lime freshly slaked to a powder. Allow same to dry slowly and heat as customary.

CEMENT FOR MACHINE PARTS.

A good cement for machine parts consists of a compound of gutta percha with filings of iron, steel, copper or brass, or as a substitute for the latter, with powdered iron or copper ores.

CEMENT FOR METAL AND GLASS.

To fasten metal on glass rapidly and securely, thoroughly mix 50 parts of dried white lead with 100 parts by weight of pulverized white litharge and stir it to a plastic mass by mixing in 1 part of copal lacquer and 3 parts of boiled linseed oil. The process of cementing is easy. Coat the lower surface of the metal with the cement, press upon the glass and remove the excess of cement with a proper tool. Then cement dries quickly and becomes very hard.

CEMENT FOR METAL LETTERS.

A cement for fastening metal letters upon wood, metal, glass, etc., is compounded of 5 parts of oil of turpentine, 5 parts of boiled linseed oil, 15 parts of copal varnish and 5 parts of glue. The dissolution of the glue is effected by putting a pound into a water bath. When this is dissolved, add into the mixture 10 parts of slaked lime.

(2) Compound together 7 parts of tar oil, 10 of plaster of paris and roman cement, 8 of caoutchouc dissolved in tar oil, 5 of linseed oil. Boil with litharge and 15 parts of copal varnish, prepared with gum lac.

(3) Compound together 5 parts of linseed oil boiled with litharge, 5 parts oil of turpentine and 15 parts of a varnish made of white resin and sandarac. To this 5 parts of marine glue are to be added and on the dissolution of this mixture in a water bath 10 parts of white lead and flake white are to be added.

(4) Compound together 10 parts of ochre or washed clay, 2 parts of powdered isinglass, 5 of sifted iron filings, 5 parts oil of turpentine with 15 parts copal varnish made ready with the addition of resin.

CEMENT FOR METAL MOUNTINGS ON PORCELAIN, BRASS, ETC.

For fastening metal mountings on metal, glass, etc.,

dissolve in water 2 parts of high grade glue. Heat the solution over a coal fire and then add ½ part of Venetian turpentine and 1 part of good linseed oil varnish. After the articles have been cemented they should remain tied together for from 40 to 60 hours.

CEMENT FOR METAL PARTS ON GLASS LAMPS, ETC.

A cement for fastening the metal parts on glass lamps, etc., is composed of 20 parts plaster of paris, 20 parts of water, 16 parts of strong lime, 12 parts of resin. Boil the resin with the lime until it is completely dissolved, and when cold, it forms a solid and tenacious mass. Dilute this by the addition of water and carefully work in the plaster of paris. You can dissolve this in petroleum.

CEMENT FOR PACKING STEAM PISTONS.

A cement for packing stuffing boxes and pistons for steam engines is composed of

10 parts Copper, Zinc or Lead Filings,
1 part Powdered Graphite,
1 part Silicate of Magnesia,
2 parts Gutta-percha,
1 part Sulphur,
5 parts Caoutchouc.

If this cement is to be exposed to the direct action of the fire or place where it will encounter a high degree of heat, asbestos should be added to the mixture.

CEMENT FOR PIPE CONDUITS UNEXPOSED TO HEAT.

Cement for pipe conduits which are not exposed to heat is made of

10 parts Iron Fillings,
1 part Sal-ammoniac,
1 part Sulphur,
4 parts Caoutchouc,
1 part Gutta-percha.

CEMENT FOR PUNCTURED TIRES.

A cement for punctured bicycle tires is composed as follows: Bisulphide of carbon, 100 parts; gutta-percha, 20 parts; caoutchouc, 40 parts; isinglass, 10 parts.

CEMENT FOR REPAIRING IRON PANS.

Take 1 part of fine black lead, 2 parts sulphur; place the sulphur in an iron pan, elevating it from the fire until the commencement of melting, at which time the black lead is to be added. Mix thoroughly until it is well melted and then pour out upon a smooth stone or iron plate. After it is cool, break it into small pieces. A large enough amount of this composition when put upon the crack of an iron pot needing repairing can be soldered with a hot iron just as sheets are soldered. When there is a little hole in the pot, hammer a copper rivet therein and then solder over it with this cement.

CEMENT FOR RESERVOIR JOINTS.

(1) For cementing steam joints of iron and water joints, mix iron filings with sulphuric acid, diluted with 1 part acid to 30 parts of water or with wine vinegar, and pack the compound into the joints.

(2) Make a paste composed of 1 part green vitriol, 2 parts iron filings and wine vinegar.

CEMENT FOR SMALL ARTICLES.

An improved cement for small iron articles is made as follows: Take 2 parts sulphur and 1 part by weight of fine black lead, put the sulphur in an old iron pan, holding it over the fire until it begins to melt, then add the lead; stir well until all is melted, then pour out on an iron plate, or smooth stone. When cool, break into small pieces. A sufficient quantity of this compound being placed upon the crack of the iron pot to be mended, can be soldered by a hot iron in the same manner as a tinsmith solders his sheets. If there is a small hole in the pot, drive a copper rivet in it, and then solder it with the cement.

CEMENT FOR STEAM BOILERS.

Red or white leaf in oil 4 parts, iron borings 3 parts, makes a soft cement for steam boilers.

CEMENT FOR STEAM PIPES.

For a cement for steam pipes, which will not require the removal of the injured piece, take 5 pounds of paris white, 5 pounds yellow ochre, 10 pounds of litharge, 5 pounds red lead, and 4 pounds black oxide manganese. Mix with great thoroughness and add a small quantity of asbestos and boiled oil. This composition will set hard in from two to five hours.

(2) A cement for steam pipes is made of

10 parts Iron Filings,
1 part Sulphur,
2 parts Caoutchouc,
1 part Gutta-percha.

CEMENT FOR STONE WORK.

A fine cement for stone work is made of equal parts of resin, yellow wax and Venetian red, mixed up together while in a melted condition.

CEMENT FOR STOVE JOINTS.

Cement for cementing joints or cracks in iron stoves is composed of clay, salt, sand, coarse iron filings and cow-hair with fresh blood.

Another good cement is composed of salt with water, clay and beechwood-ash.

CEMENT FOR STOVES.

A mixture in the form of a cement which may be used to stop the cracks in stoves so the smoke will not pass through is composed of glycerine and litharge mixed to a paste. Another receipt is to take equal parts of sulphur and white lead, with about a sixth of borax, incorporating them so as to form one homogeneous mass. When going to apply it, wet it with strong sulphuric acid, and place a thin layer of it between the two pieces of iron, which should then be pressed together.

(2) For stove cement use pulverized clay, 8 parts; fine iron filings, 4 parts; peroxide of manganese, 2 parts, sea salt, 1 part; borax, 1 part. Thoroughly pulverize, dry and mix. When required for use, make up the required quantity for immediate use into a thick putty with water.

CEMENT FOR TIN AND GLASS.

For cementing tin and glass together a putty of pure white or red lead is recommended. Marine glue is also used. A tolerable elastic cement may be made by warming common coal tar until soft, and then mixing rather stiff with Portland cement.

CEMENT FOR TINFOIL.

For a cement which will attach tinfoil to paper or other articles, dissolve caustic soda in twice its weight of water; add rye flour until no more of the flour will dissolve, adding a little water and stirring all the time. To the paste thus prepared add a few drops of Venice turpentine, liquefying the turpentine by gentle heat. The paste thus made will firmly fix tinfoil.

CEMENT FOR WATER PIPES.

A cement for joining cast-iron water pipes is made as follows: Intimately mix 8 parts white lead, 2 parts litharge, 1 part of colophony and 24 parts Roman cement. Stir this into a plastic mass with old linseed oil, kept boiling together with one-half its weight of colophony until the dissolution of the latter.

(2) Melt together tallow and colophony, stirring into the melted mass sufficient finely sifted gypsum to give it the consistency desired. Compound together equal parts of potters' clay, Roman cement, clay and burned lime, all dried separately and ground fine. The mixture is to be worked together with linseed oil.

CEMENT FOR ZINC AND GLASS.

An inexpensive cement for uniting zinc with glass may be made as follows: One pound of shellac dissolved in 1 pint of alcohol, with one-twentieth its volume of a solution of gutta-percha in bisulphide of carbon, will dry quickly. A slow-drying one may be made thus: Two ounces of thick glue solution, 1 ounce linseed oil varnish, or ¾ ounce Venetian turpentine. Boil together.

(2) A cement to unite zinc strongly to glass is thus made: One pound of shellac dissolved in one pint of alcohol, with one-twentieth its volume of a solution of gutta-percha in bisulphide of carbon. It dries quickly.

CEMENT FOR ZINC ORNAMENTS.

A colored cement to repair zinc ornaments is made by thoroughly stirring together fine whiting with soda water solution of 33 degrees Be, to which zinc dust is added, the whole being stirred to a thick, plastic mass, which hardens in from six to eight hours and acquires an unusual calidity and a gray color. If it is desired that it should have a lustrous white color after hardening it can be polished with an agate.

CEMENT—GASFITTERS'.

Gasfitters' cement consists of 4½ parts of resin, 1 part of wax, and 3 parts of Venitian red.

CEMENT—GLASS.

Is composed of tin (2 parts), lead (3 parts), bismuth (2½ parts).

CEMENT—GROUVELLES' OIL.

Grouvelles' oil cement is made by intimately mixing 2½ parts of white lead, 1 part of red lead, 2 parts of perfectly dry clay, finely pulverized with boiled linseed oil.

CEMENT IMPERVIOUS TO OIL.

A cement impervious to oil, and, therefore, useful to mend kerosene lamps, is made by taking 3 parts of resin boiled with 5 parts of water and 1 part of caustic soda. Mix with half its weight of plaster of paris. This sets in one hour.

CEMENTING BRASS ON GLASS.

Puscher recommends a resin soap for this purpose, made by boiling 1 part caustic soda, 3 parts of colophonium (resin) in 5 parts of water, and kneading into it half the quantity of plaster of paris. This cement is useful for fastening the brass top on glass lamps, as it is very strong, is not acted upon by petroleum, bears heat very well, and hardens in one-half or three-quarters of an hour.

By substituting zinc white, white lead, or air-slaked lime for plaster of paris, it hardens more slowly. Water only attacks the surface of this cement.

Wiederhold recommends, for the same purpose, a fusible metal, composed of 4 parts lead, 2 parts tin, and 2½ parts bismuth, which melts at 212 degrees Fahrenheit. The melted metal is poured into the capsule, the glass pressed into it, and then allowed to cool slowly in a warm place.

CEMENTING CRACKS IN STOVES.

A paste of equal parts of sifted ashes, clay and salt, and a little water, cements cracks in stoves and ovens.

CEMENTING GLASS INTO METAL.

(1) Melt carefully 40 parts of white wax, 80 of colcothar and 160 parts by weight of finely pulverized colophony. Add to the mass when melting 20 parts by weight of Venetian turpentine. The mass is to be removed from the fire and the finished cement mixed until cold with a wooden spatula. This cement is to be applied when warm.

(2) Compound together equal quantities of finely powdered pumice and shellac and make application of same while warm.

(3) Mix 1 part of white wax and 10 parts of beech. This cement will be found especially valuable for fastening metal or glass articles for optical glasses, so that in polishing they remain fixed.

(4) Take a good grade of sealing wax, taking pains that same is not too brittle. If there is any brittle-

ness, remove same with a little Venetian turpentine. When the glass is cemented in a metallic case, both should be heated to the melting point of the sealing wax.

CEMENTING IRON TO IRON.

A cement for pieces of iron to iron which must be used soon after it is made is composed of 1 part flowers of sulphur, 2 parts sal-ammoniac, 60 parts powdered cast-iron bore chips. Stir into a stiff paste by the addition of water.

CEMENTING IRON TO WOOD.

To cement iron to wood or stone, melt together 1 part of wax and 4 parts of black pitch, and mix into the melted mass 1 part of brick dust.

CEMENTING KNIVES AND FORKS IN SILVER HANDLES.

Two parts of pitch are to be melted and then 1 part of brick dust is stirred in. The cavity in the handle is filled with this compound and the tang of the blade is then forced in.

CEMENTING KNIVES AND FORKS IN THEIR HANDLES.

(1) To cement knives and forks in their handles, compound together 2 parts of pulverized colophony and 1 part of brick dust. The cavity in the handle is to be filled with this compound and then you force in the heated tang of the blade.

(2) Another cement which is equally good for this purpose and is applied in the same manner is made by melting together 1 part of sulphur and 4 parts of colophony; iron filings, brick dust or fine sand being mixed into the melted mass.

CEMENTING METAL PLATES ON WOODEN BOXES.

To cement metal plates on wooden boxes, melt together 1 part linseed oil and 6 parts resin and mix into the melted mass ½ part of plaster of paris and 1 part of burnt ochre.

CEMENTING RUBBER OR GUTTA PERCHA TO METAL.

Rubber, or gutta percha, may be cemented to metal by the following process: Take pulverized shellac and dissolve in ten times its weight of pure ammonia. In three days the mixture will be of the required consistency. The ammonia penetrates the rubber, and enables the shellac to take a firm hold; but as it all evaporates in time, the rubber is immovably fastened to the metal, and neither gas nor water will remove it.

CEMENTING STEAM PIPES.

The cement is composed of 5 pounds Paris white, 5 pounds yellow ochre, 10 pounds litharge, 5 pounds red lead, and 4 pounds black oxide of manganese, these various materials being mixed with great thoroughness, a small quantity of asbestos and boiled oil being afterward added. The composition as thus prepared will set hard in from two to five hours, and possess the advantage of not being subject to expansion and contraction to such an extent as to cause leakage afterward, and its efficiency in places difficult of access is of special importance. This is a cement of specially valuable properties for steam pipes, in filling up small leaks, such as a blow-hole in a casting, without the necessity of removing the injured place.

CEMENTING THIN METAL SHEETS.

To cement thin metal sheets, dissolve isinglass cut into little pieces in a small amount of water at a moderate heat, small portions of nitric acid being added, the determination of the proper proportions generally being gained by experiment. Great care should be taken about the amount of nitric acid used. If not enough is taken, the cement will not adhere well; while if too much, the cement will require even weeks for drying.

CEMENTING WITH COPPER AMALGAM.

To cement articles with copper amalgam, first brighten them with acid, then heat to from 176 to 194 degrees Fahrenheit, and after the application of the amalgam, firmly press them together. The adhesion of the parts is as firm as if they were soldered.

CEMENT—IRON.

A good cement for iron railing top, iron grating, etc., is made of equal parts of white lead and sulphur with about 1-6 part of borax, these three substances being intimately mixed, forming a homogeneous mass. Before application of this compound, moisten it with strong sulphuric acid, placing a thin layer of it between the two pieces of iron, which are pressed together at once. It will take a period of five days for this to become perfectly dry, at which time all traces of the cement will have disappeared, the job looking as though it had been welded.

(2) The "boss" cement for iron is the plain "rust joint," made with iron filings and water, without any acids or sulphur, etc., which the books direct. When well caulked into the joint, if fine filings are used, it is possible to crack the hub of a pipe by the expansion of the filings. This can be put in any place where the filings have a chance to wedge themselves as they rust. The recipe is simple, iron filings or turnings and water calked into the crack to be filled.

CEMENT—IRON.

Iron cement which will stand red heat is composed of Hessian crucibles 1 part, iron filings 4 parts. Mix these ingredients and wet them with salt water, taking pains not to add too large a quantity of salt, for if this is none the salt would fuse and run from the joints. When this cement is used for joining pipes designed for being laid in the fire, it is placed between the flange of the pipes and pressed together by screws. You can ouly heat it when it is hard and dry.

CEMENT—IRON, FOR HIGH TEMPERATURES.

An iron cement for high temperatures is composed of:

(1) Iron filings, 20 parts; lime powder, 45; borax, 5; common salt, 5; permanganate of potash, 10. The borax and salts are dissolved in water and are then mixed with the two first-named ingredients as quickly as possible, and used. This cement changes at a white heat to a glassy mass, which is perfectly airproof.

(2) Permanganate, 25 parts; zinc white, 25; borax, 5. These are treated with a solution of soluble glass, and used at once. This cement must be left to dry slowly, and then it will resist the highest temperature.

CEMENT—IRON STOVE.

For cementing iron stoves, make a paste of wood ashes, 10 parts; burned lime, 4 parts; clay, 10 parts.

CEMENT—JEWELERS'.

A receipt for jewelers' cement, often called Armenian cement, is as follows: Five pieces of gum mastic, about as large as a large pea, are dissolved in a sufficient quantity of spirits of wine to make the mass liquid. Separately, isinglass which has been softened in water (though none of the water must be used) is dissolved in rum, enough being dissolved to make a 2-ounce phial of a very tenacious glue; 2 little pieces of gum ammoniac being added, which must be rubbed or ground until its dissolution. The entire mass then to be mixed to a sufficient heat. This cement is to be kept in a phial closely stoppered, and said phial is to be placed in boiling water when it is to be used. This cement will unite almost all substances, being practically the only cement for glass and polished steel.

CEMENT—JOINT.

(1) For a joint cement, mix equal parts of red lead and white lead, adding enough boiled linseed-oil to give it the right consistency.

(2) Make a soft putty of finely-powdered red lead with ground lead.

CEMENT—METAL.

Is composed of antimony (3 parts), lead (8 parts), bismuth (1 part).

CEMENT—OIL.

The oil cements require two or three years to set. The best cement of this kind is composed of pure white lead ground in linseed oil varnish, and kept from the air in close stoppered bottles or packages.

CEMENT—RUST FOR IRON.

Rust cement for iron is made as follows: Wrought-iron filings, 65 parts; sal-ammoniac, 2½ parts; sulphur (flour), 1½ parts; sulphuric acid, 1 part. The solid ingredients are mixed dry, sulphuric acid diluted with sufficient water being then added. This cement dries after two or three days, and unites with the iron, making a very resisting and solid mass.

CEMENTS—RUST-JOINT.

(1) Cement for setting quickly: 1 part (by weight) sal-ammoniac in powder; 2 parts flour of sulphur; 80 parts iron borings; made to a paste with water.

(2) Cement for slowly setting, but better than the above if it has time to set, is made from the same material but in different proportions; 2 parts sal-ammoniac; 1 part flour of sulphur; 200 parts iron borings.

CEMENT—STEPHENSON'S OIL.

Stephenson's oil cement, which must be used shortly after it is made, is composed of lime fallen to a powder 1 part, fine sand 1 part, litharge 2 parts, stirred into a paste with hot linseed oil.

CEMENT—"STONE."

To make "Stone" cement, take an ordinary resin and powder coarsely so as to melt easily; use of the resin, 1 ounce; yellow wax, 1 ounce; Venetian red, 1 ounce. Melt the resin, then add the wax, and lastly, stir in the Venetian red. This cement may be "pulled" into sticks and used by melting into place with a hot iron on the piece of iron or stone, or both, if convenient, may be heated hot enough to melt the cement; then, if held in position until the cement is cold, they will be found strongly fixed together.

CEMENT—STOVE.

Litharge, 2 parts; powdered slaked lime, 1 part; sand, 1 part. Mix the mass with a sufficient quantity of hot linseed oil varnish to form a stiff paste. This cement must be used while fresh and warm.

CHILLING IRON VERY HARD.

To chill iron very hard, use a liquid made as follows: Soft water, 10 gallons; salt, 1 peck; oil of vitriol, ½ pint; saltpetre, ½ pound; prussiate of potash, ¼ pound; cyanide of potash, ¼ pound. Heat the iron a cherry red and dip as usual; if not sufficiently hard repeat the process.

CHLORIDE OF GOLD.

Chloride of gold is prepared by the dissolution of finely laminated gold in aqua regia.

CHLORIDE OF PLATINUM.

Chloride of platinum is prepared much like chloride of gold, but the aqua regia used should be made of 5 parts of hydro-chloric acid and 3 parts nitric acid.

CHLORIDE OF ZINC.

Chloride of zinc is obtained by the introduction of zinc into hydro-chloric acid.

CHROME YELLOW.

Chrome yellow is a precipitation made by mixing a solution of potassium chromate with lead nitric.

CHRYSOCHALK.

Chrysochalk is a copper-zinc alloy composed of

90 parts Copper,
7 9-10 parts Zinc.

CHRYSORIN.

Chrysorin is a copper-zinc alloy composed of either

72 parts Copper,
28 parts Zinc,
or
66 7-10 parts Copper,
33 3-10 parts Zinc.

CHURCH BELLS—REPAIRING.

To repair cracked church-bells so that their tone will be as good as new, put a furnace in the middle of the bell so as to heat same, and after fusion of the edges of the crack, pour new bell-metal in same. The wall of the bell must be blocked up in order to prevent the escape of liquid metal.

CLEANING BRASS.

Acids should never be employed in cleaning brass, as the metal soon becomes dull after such treatment. The application of olive oil and very fine tripoli, followed by a washing with soap and water, constitutes the best method of polishing and preserving the brilliancy.

(2) Use sweet oil and whiting.

(3) To clean brass, rub the surface of the metal with rotten-stone and sweet oil, then rub off with a piece of cotton flannel, and polish with soft leather. A solution of oxalic acid rubbed over tarnished brass soon removes the tarnish, rendering the metal bright. The acid must be washed off with water, and the brass rubbed with whiting and soft leather. A mixture of muriatic acid and alum dissolved in water imparts a golden color to brass articles that are steeped in it a few seconds.

(4) The government method prescribed for clean-

ing brass, and its use in all the United States arsenals, is claimed to be the best in the world. The plan is to make a mixture of one part common nitric and one-half part sulphuric acid in a stone jar, having also ready a pail of fresh water and a box of sawdust. The articles to be treated are dipped into the acid, then removed into the water, and finally rubbed with the sawdust. This immediately changes them to a brilliant color. If the brass has become greasy, it is first dipped in a strong solution of potash and soda in warm water; this cuts the grease, so that the acid has free power to act.

(5) In cases where brass cannot be successfully cleaned with oxalic acid it should be rubbed with potash lye and then plunged in a mixture of equal parts of sulphuric acid, nitric acid and water, and then washed, rinsed, dried and polished.

(8) To remove the stains of iodide potassa and aqua ammonia stains off brass, scour with a mixture of ammonia water, alcohol, and chalk. For delicate work the chalk should be finely levigated. For heavy work powdered bath brick, rotten stone, red brick dust, or Tripoli in sweet oil may be rubbed on with a flannel, and the article polished with leather. The government method has been to dip the article in a mixture of two parts nitric acid and one part sulphuric acid, immediately removing to water, and finally rubbing with sawdust. Grease is removed with alkali.

CLEANING BRONZE.

To clean bronze: Take 1 ounce of oxalic acid, 6 ounces rottenstone, 1 or 2 ounces gum arabic in powder, 10 ounces sweet oil, and a sufficient quantity of water to make a paste. Apply a small portion to the pan, and polish with a flannel or piece of soft leather.

CLEANING BRONZE FIXTURES.

Boil them in ordinary soap boilers' lye, rinse with water and roll in sawdust or bran. When the bronze is pressed mix the lye with common salt and brush the article thoroughly, allowing no water to touch the back.

CLEANING CHANDELIERS.

To clean chandeliers or gas fixtures they should be taken apart and the separate parts boiled for a few minutes in a sharp lye, followed by their cleansing with a soft brush. They should next be drawn through a strong solution of potassium cyanide, then washed in a large boiler with hot water, dried in clean sawdust and then polished with chamois skin. In some cases parts should be lacquered after they have been put together again.

CLEANING COINS AND MEDALS.

To clean coins and medals a mildly concentrated solution of potassium cyanide is recommended. When medals or other small silver objects are to be cleaned, three vessels or glasses should be placed side by side, two of which are filled with water and the third with a solution of potassium cyanide. The object to be cleaned is to be taken up with brass tweezers and dipped in the vessel containing the potassium cyanide. This will cause the brown or dirty yellow coating on same to vanish at once. The medals, or other objects, are then to be rapidly rinsed in the secónd and third tumblers, and then dried with a linen cloth. Articles of a larger size, such as spoons, candlesticks, chafing-dishes, etc., are treated by wetting the yellow places with a small tuft of cotton thoroughly moistened with a solution of potassium cyanide, then washed and dried. The modus operandi is the same for gilded articles.

OLEANING GOLDEN-BRONZE.

To cleanse bronze by oil, tallow, fat or other grease, boil it in an infusion of ashes and clean with a soft brush dipped in a fluid consisting of equal parts of nitric acid, alum and water. Dry each piece with a rag, and heat slightly. When it is desired to clean clock pendulums and free them from what is technically known as "mercury dust," they should be heated slightly and the stain touched with a brush dipped in nitric acid. Then rub with a linen rag and heat moderately a second time.

CLEANING MARBLE.

To clean marble mix 2 parts of common soda, 1 part powdered pumice stone and 1 part powdered chalk with water. Rub it well over the marble and then wash the marble with soap and water.

CLEANING OLD BRASS.

To clean articles of antique brass, such as sword-hilts, mountings, etc., dip them in a compound of ½ part sulphuric acid and 1 part nitric acid. After a brief immersion take them out, rinse thoroughly in cold water, dry in sawdust and then polish with finely pulverized Vienna lime.

CLEANING POLISHING LEATHER.

To clean polishing leather prepare a weak solution of soda in warm water, rub soap on polishing leather and allow same to soak for several hours. Then wash thoroughly and rinse in a solution of soda and yellow soap water to keep it soft. If washed in water alone the leather becomes too hard to use, but the small amount of soap remaining in the fibre of the leather penetrates it, making it soft as silk. When it has been rinsed, wring the weather in a coarse towel and dry quickly. When dry, pull it in every direction and brush well. This will give a very soft leather.

CLEANING SCREWS OF RUST.

To clean screws that are not large enough to be treated separately, put them in a small box, pour a little oil over them and shake for a minute. Next place cotton waste in the box and shake again for a minute. Then put a handful of sawdust in the box and shake again for a minute, removing sawdust by sifting it from the screws in a fine sieve.

CLEANING SILVER DIAL PLATES.

To clean silver dial plates of clocks, which have lost their bright surface from the effect of smoke or sulphurous vapors, make pulverized tartar into a paste with water. Some of this paste is taken on a bristly brush and the dial plate is rubbed, being whirled until the silvering assumes again its original whiteness and lustre. Then the dial plate is to be washed with clean water and dried by mildly patting it with a cloth, the final step being its exposure to a moderate heat for a few minutes.

CLEANING SILVER ORNAMENTS.

To clean silver ornaments, first wash article in a bath of soda lye, then use either a boiling hot solution of tartar, or enwrap them with zinc wire, boiling them in a fluid consisting of 1 part of borax dissolved in 10 parts of water.

CLEANING SOLDER FROM OLD FILES.

The best way to clean solder from old files is to soak the file in raw muriatic acid for twenty-four hours, and you will have almost a new file.

CLEANING TINWARE.

To clean tinware use Canton flannel, with a little alcohol sprinkled on it, and some whiting.

(2) To clean tinware which has been stained by using acid when soldering, rub the article first with rotten stone and sweet oil, then finish with whiting and a piece of soft leather.

CLICHE METAL

Is composed of tin (36 parts), lead (50 parts), cadmium (22 5-10 parts); or, tin (48 parts), lead (32½ parts), cadmium (10½ parts), bismuth (9 parts).

COATING ALUMINUM.

The processes ordinarily used for covering metals with zinc, tin and lead have not, up to the present, appeared to be applicable to aluminum. When a plate of aluminum, mechanically or chemically cleaned, is immersed in melted tin, zinc or lead, these metals slide over the surface of the aluminum without alloying therewith. In order to fix the above-named metals, it suffices to submit the surface of the aluminum to a vigorous brushing in the metallic bath. For this purpose a steel brush or any other analogous instrument may be used. Under such circumstances the aluminum becomes covered with a regular layer of the melted metal. The success of the operation was due, it appears, not to the want of affinity of the aluminum for the metals in question, but to the immediate formation in contact with the air, of a thin stratum of oxide of aluminum, which friction removes.

(2) To coat aluminum with other metals: Dip the aluminum in a solution of caustic potash or soda, or of hydro-chloric acid, until bubbles of gas make their appearance on its surface, whereupon it is dipped into a solution of corrosive sublimate to amalgamate its surface. After a second dipping into the potash solution until bubbles of gas are evolved, the metal is placed in a solution of a salt of the desired metal—for instance, bluestone for copper, and lunar caustic for silver. A film of the metal is rapidly formed, and is so firmly adherent that, in the case of silver, gold or copper, the plate can be rolled out or polished. When coating with gold or copper, it is best to first apply a layer of silver. When thus treated the aluminum may be soldered with ordinary zinc solder.

COATING IRON WITH COPPER.

(1) Iron can be coppered by dipping it into melted copper, the surface of which is protected by a melted layer of cryolite and phosphoric acid.

(2) To coat iron with copper consists in dipping the article in a solution of oxalate of copper and bicarbonate of soda, dissolved in 10 or 15 parts of water acidified with some organic acid.

COATING SURFACES WITH GLASS.

The following is the method for coating metal surfaces with glass, which may be found to answer various purposes. Take about 125 parts (by weight) of ordinary flint glass fragments, 20 parts of carbonate of soda, and 12 parts of boracic acid, and melt. Pour the fused mass out on some cold surface, as of stone of metal, and pulverize when cooled off. Make a mixture of this powder with silicate of soda.

COATING WITH ZINC.

For coating with zinc large pieces that cannot conveniently be put in a bath: Mix powdered zinc with linseed oil and a dryer so as to make a kind of paint that can be applied with a brush. One coating will prevent oxidation, but two are advisable.

COATING CAST-BRONZE.

To coat cast-bronze goods use a lacquer consisting of shellac dissolved in alcohol with a little camphor added. Another good lacquer consists of 1 part shallac dissolved in 8 or 10 of alcohol, to which the addition is made of 1 to 4 parts of camphor, and rubbed up with a few drops of lavender.

COATING CAST-IRON A GLOSSY BLACK.

To coat cast-iron a glossy black color that will stand washing and heat, take oil of turpentine and add to it strong sulpuric acid, drop by drop, while stirring, until a syrupy precipitate is formed and no more of it is produced on further addition of a drop of acid. The liquid is now repeatedly washed away with water, every time renewed after a good stirring, until the water does not exhibit any more acid reaction with blue litmus paper. The precipitate is next brought upon a cloth filter, and after all the water has run off the syrup is fit for use. This thickish deposit is painted over the iron with a brush; if it happens to be too stiff, it is previously diluted with some oil of turpentine. Immediately after the iron has been painted, the paint is burnt in by a gentle heat, and, after cooling, the black surface is rubbed over with a piece of linen stuff dipped and moistened with linseed oil.

COATING IRON WITH COPPER.

One process of coating iron with copper consists of dipping the articles into a melted mixture of one pint of chloride or fluroide of copper and five or six parts of cryolite, and a little chloride of barium. If the article when immersed is connected with the negative pole of a battery it hastens the process.

COBALTOUS CHLORIDE.

Cobaltous chloride is obtained in blue crystalline scales by heating the metal in chloric acid.

COLCOTHAR.

Colcothar, otherwise known as sesqui oxide iron, is a by-product in the manufacture of sulphuric acid from the solution of ferrous sulphate.

COLORING BRASS.

The pieces to be operated on must first be slightly corroded by placing them for a minute or two in dilute sulphuric acid. They are next rubbed with sand and water, washed and dried. Brown of any shade is produced by dipping the pieces in some solution of a nitrate or in iron per-chloride. The shade depends on the concentration of the solution. A chocolate color is obtained by roasting with moist red iron oxide and polishing with a small quantity of galena. Black brass for optical instruments is obtained by dipping the brass objects in a mixture consisting of solutions of gold or platinum and stannic nitrate.

To very handsomely color brass black, mix 180 grams carbonate of copper, 400 grams aqua ammonia, and 400 grams water. The cleansed brass articles can be dipped into this mixture, frequently withdrawn to inspect them, rinsed in water, and dried in sawdust, and the process is repeated twice; the articles are then freely rubbed with a little linseed oil; the color will then be that of ebony. The oil process of silver is somewhat dearer, and another of dipping, hot, into nitrate of copper, is ruinous to delicately soldered articles, wherefore the first mentioned method is preferable.

A steel color is developed on brass by using a boiling solution of arsenic chloride, while a careful application of a concentrated solution of sodium sulphide causes a blue coloration. Black, being generally used for optical instruments, is obtained from a solution of platinum chloride, to which tin nitrate has been added. In Japan the brass is bronzed by using a boiling solution of copper sulphate, alum and verdigris.

COLORING BRASS VIOLET.

To give a violet color to brass dissolve 4½ ounces of sodium hyposulphide in 1 quart of water. Then dissolve 1 ounce 3¾ drachms of crystallized sugar of lead in another quart of water and mix the solutions. This mixture is to be heated to 176 degrees Fahrenheit, the articles plunged in same and moved around constantly. The first color which will appear on the brass subjected to this bath will be gold-yellow. This will, however, soon be replaced by violet, and if the article remains longer in the bath it will become green.

(2) Colors of similar lustre are also secured by the dissolution of 1 quart of water of 2 11-100 ounces pulverized tartar, and also by the dissolution in ½ pint of water of 1 ounce of chloride of tin. These solutions are to be mixed, heated and the clear mixture is poured into a solution of 6 34-100 ounces of sodium-hyposulphide in 1 pint of water. This mixture is to be heated to 176 degrees Fahrenheit and the pickled brass objects plunged therein.

COLORING COPPER BLUE-BLACK.

To give copper a blue-black color dip it in a hot solution of 11¼ drachms of liver of sulphur in 1 quart of water, stirring same constantly but gently. If a blue-gray shade is desired the solution must be diluted more.

COLORING COPPER BROWN.

The method of coloring copper brown is as follows: As a corrosive, a liquid is used which is produced as follows: Ten portions by weight of spirits of ammonia mixed with an equal amount of vinegar, so that a piece of blue litmus paper dipped into it will be colored red, and to this mixture, which is acetate of ammonia, are to be added 5 parts of verdigris and 3 parts of ammonia. By means of this mixture large objects that you wish to color should, after being carefully cleaned of grease and rust, be painted with a soft brush and then left to dry in a warm room. By repeating this application with the brush, you can get the brown in any shade you like. Small objects should be boiled in the liquid, and during the boiling should be stirred with a tin or copper spoon. After securing the desired color they are to be washed in hot water and subsequently dried in sawdust.

COLORING SOFT SOLDER.

In order that solder employed for soldering copper may have the same color, the first step in preparation is making a saturated solution of pure sulphate of copper and the application of the same to the solder. When the solder is touched with an iron or steel wire it becomes colored with a copper film which may be augmented at pleasure by repeated dampening with the solution of copper and touching with the wire. If it is desired that the soldering should show a yellow color, 2 parts of solution of sulphate of copper should be compounded with 1 part of saturated solution of sulphate of zinc, the mixture applied to the coppered place and all rubbed with a zinc rod. Should it be desired to gild the soldered place, copper it in accordance with the above description and coat with a solution of isinglass or gum and scatter bronze powder over it. This forms a surface which can be polished when the gum is dried.

(2) When brass is soldered with soft solder, the difference in color is so marked as to direct attention to the spot mended. The following is the method of

coloring soft solder: First prepare a saturated solution of sulphate of copper (bluestone) in water, and apply some of this on the end of a stock to the solder. On touching it with a steel or iron wire it becomes coppered, and by repeating the experiment the deposit of copper may be made thicker and darker. To give the solder a yellowish color, mix one part of a saturated solution of sulphate of copper, apply this to the coppered spot, and rub it with a zinc rod. The color can be still further improved by applying gilt powder and polishing.

On gold jewelry, or colored gold, the solder is first coppered as above, then a thin coat of gum or isinglass solution is applied and bronze powder dusted over it, which can be polished after the gum is dry, and made very smooth and brilliant; or the article may be electro-plated with gold, and then it will all have the same color.

On silverware the coppered spots of solder are rubbed with silvering powder, or polished with the brush and then carefully scratched with the scratch brush, then finally polished.

COLORING SOLDER.

Dissolve five cents' worth of sulphate of copper in just as little water as possible. Solder smoothly, polish very bright with a cloth, and with a stick wet the solder with the solution and it will turn copper-color. It can be improved by polishing with bronze powder.

(2) To color tin solder yellow, it is best first to prepare a saturated solution of copper vitrol in water, dip an emery stick into it and touch the soldered part with it. Then take a piece of wire and touch the part again with this, by which a coppering takes place. To turn this yellow, take one part of a saturated solution of vitriol of zinc in water mixed with two parts of a copper vitriol solution, brush the coppered spot and touch with a zinc rod. A brass precipitate will result. The color may be still further improved by burnishing with gold powder and polishing with polisher.

COLORING SOLDER LIKE COPPER.

When copper is soldered and the solder is to be colored like the surrounding copper, this can be done by moistening the solder with a saturated solution of vitriol of copper, and then touching the solder with an iron or steel wire. A thin skin of copper is precipitated, which can be thickened by repeating the process several times.

COLORING ZINC.

Beautiful and durable rainbow colorations are imparted to zinc by a very simple process. The zinc to be thus treated may be in any form, cast or sheet, the special requisites being that it be pure, dry, polished or filed; the coloration is the more brilliant according as the materials of the bath are pure, and thus the best effects are obtained with chemically pure reagents. The bath consists of 30 grammes tartrate of copper, 40 grammes caustic potash and 400 grammes distilled water. On subjecting the zinc to the action of this kind of bath for a couple of minutes it appears an agreeable violet; for three minutes, a deep blue; four and one-half minutes, green; six and one-half minutes, a golden yellow; eight and one-half minutes, purple violet.

(2) To give zinc a black color dip the article in a boiling solution of 3 17-100 ounces sal-ammoniac and 5 64-100 ounces pure green vitriol in 4½ quarts of water. The loose black precipitation on the articles is removed by means of a brush and the article is again dipped in the hot solution and then held over a coal fire until the evaporation of ammonia salt. A repetition of this three or four times gives a black coating of tenacious adherence. By the surpension of zinc in a nickel bath, slightly acidulated with sulphuric acid, a blue-black coating is formed without the employment of a current. The same result can be secured by dipping the zinc articles in a solution of 2 11-10 ounces of a double sulphate of ammonium and nickel, and a like amount of sal-ammoniac in 1 quart of water. The article assumes first a dark yellow color, and then be-

comes brown, purple-violet and indigo-blue in succession, and will stand a slight brushing with a scratch brush and polishing.

(3) The various colors on zinc are obtained as follows: To give it a reddish-brown color, rub with a solution of chloride of copper in liquid ammonia. To give it a yellow-brown shade rub with a solution of chloride of copper in vinegar. To give it a copper-red color immerse the article in a bath of chloride of copper and dissolve in spirits of sal-ammoniac. To give it a yellowish tone add crystallized verdigris. To give it a bronze color rub it with a paste of pipeclay, to which has been added a solution of 1 part tartar, 2 parts crystallized soda and 2 parts crystallized verdigris.

COMPOUND FOR HARDENING STEEL.

A valuable compound for hardening steel consists of:

1-3 Resin,
1-3 Ammonium Chloride,
1-3 Borax,
also a trace of Silicic Acid.

COPPERING SHEET IRON.

Clean the article thoroughly by a treatment in a bath of muriatic acid, 1 part; water, 4 parts, to remove all scale. Wash in hot water and tumble in sawdust wet with a solution of sulphate of copper in water, to which add as much sulphuric acid as is equal to the weight of the dry sulphate of copper. Use about two ounces of each to a gallon of water. You may also copper work that cannot be easily tumbled by dipping in the above solution hot. The work must be clean and free from grease.

COPPER NITRATE.

To form copper nitrate dissolve the copper in nitric acid, concentrating the solution in a copper kettle.

COPPER POWDER.

A copper powder is prepared by putting a strip of

sheet-zinc in a saturated solution of blue vitriol compounded with the same volume of hydro-chloric acid. The precipitation of the copper is as a fine powder, which, after the supernatant is decanted, is washed first with a weak solution of alcohol and then with a stronger one, quickly, to prevent oxidation.

COPPER RESINATE.

Copper resinate is produced as follows: Dissolve 8.55 kilogrammes of ammonia soda (18 per cent.) in 90 liters of water, and heat the whole to a boil. Now throw in gradually and in small quantities 45 kilogrammes of good resin, stir diligently, and allow to boil until the resin has completely dissolved and has transformed into resin soap. Next dissolve 23.4 kilogrammes of copper sulphate (blue vitriol) in 18 liters of boiling water, and pour the resin soap into it. The cupric resinate now separates as a thick mass, which floats on the liquid. Gather, press out in a cloth, and dry, whereupon the resinate will be ready for use.

CORRECTING BAD SMELLS.

To correct any bad smell which may arise in a tinshop place coffee in an iron vessel over the fire, close all doors and windows, and let the coffee burn until the room is thoroughly impregnated with the same. Let the room remain closed a short time, and when opened again it will be fresh and wholesome again in a few minutes. It is an excellent thing in cases of sickness, where fevers cause offensive smells.

CORROSIVE SUBLIMATE.

Corrosive sublimate is obtained by the dissolution of mercury in aqua regia. It is very poisonous.

COVERING FOR STEAM PIPES.

The following receipt produces a cheap and simple non-conducting covering for steam pipes: Four parts coal ashes, sifted through a riddle of four meshes to the inch; 1 part calcined plaster; 1 part flour; 1 part fire clay. Mix the ashes and fire-clay together to the thickness of thin mortar, in a mortar-trough; mix the calcined plaster and flour together dry, and add to it the ashes and clay as you want to use it; put it on the pipes in two coats, according to the size of the pipes. For a six-inch pipe put the first coat about 1¼ inches thick; the second coat should be about ½ inch thick. Afterwards finish with hard finish, same as applied to plastering in a room. About 2½ hours will be required to set on a hot pipe.

CRUCIBLES—THEIR PREPARATION.

A refractory crucible can be made by compounding 1 part of quartz sand with 2 parts pipe-clay. The latter, however, must be very fine.

CRYSTALLIZING TIN PLATE.

In crystallizing tin plate the figures are more or less beautiful, according to the degree of heat and relative dilution of the acid. Place the tinplate, slightly heated, over a tun of water, and rub its surfaces with a sponge dipped in a liquor composed of 4 parts of aqua fortis and 2 of distilled water, holding 1 part of common salt or salt ammoniac in solution. Whenever the crystalline spangles seem to be thoroughly brought out, the plate must be immersed in water, washed with a feather or a little cotton (taking care not to rub off the film of tin that forms the feathering), forthwith dried with a low heat, and coated with a lacquer varnish, otherwise it loses its luster in the air. If the whole surface is not plunged at once into cold water, but if it be partially cooled by sprinkling water on it, the crystallization will be finely variegated with large and small figures. Similar results will be obtained by blowing cold air through the pipe on the tinned surface, while it is just passing from the fused to the solid state.

(2) Sulphuric acid, 4 ounces; of water, 2 to 3 ounces, according to the strength of the acid; salt, 1¼ ounces. Mix. Heat the tin hot over a stove, then, with a sponge apply the mixture, then wash off directly with clean water. Dry the tin, and varnish with demar varnish.

(3) Crystallized tinplates are usually prepared from well-annealed and well-tinned charcoal iron plates, rinsing the plates with dilute nitric or nitro-muriatic acid, and then with water. The cleansed plates are dipped for a few moments into nitric acid or aqua-regia (nitric acid 1, muriatic acid 3), diluted with from one to three volumes of water heated to about 180 degrees Fah., and after a moment's exposure to this bath removed and rinsed in running water. This is repeated if necessary, until the crystals are properly developed, when the plate is finally rinsed in hot water, which causes it to dry quickly without rubbing. The plates are then oiled or lacquered to preserve them. Plates which have been heavily rolled or too quickly chilled after tinning, do not afford a good crystallized surface. Hot tannin or strong caustic soda solutions can also be used to develop the crystalline structure of tinplates.

CUIVRE FUME.

Cuivre fume is made by coloring copper blue-black with a solution of liver of sulphur, then rinsing same and brushing with a scratch brush, this making a shade lighter. The raised portions which are to show the color of copper are polished on a disk in order to remove the coloration.

CUPRIC CHLORIDE.

Cupric chloride is obtained by the dissolution of cupric oxide in hydro-chloric acid and the subsequent evaporation of same.

CUPRIC SULPHATE.

Cupric sulphate, better known as blue vitriol, or as sulphate of copper, dissolves in 4 parts of cold water. To obtain same dissolve cupric oxide in sulphuric acid.

CYANIDE OF GOLD.

Cyanide of gold is prepared by precipitation of a solution of chlorate of gold with a solution of cyanide of potassium.

DEAD BLACK FINISH ON COPPER.

To give a dead black finish to copper brush same with a compound of 1 part platinum chloride and 5 of water, and, after drying, rub with a flannel rag wet with a drop of oil. The copper can also be immersed in a solution of manganese or nitrate of copper and dried over a coal fire. This operation is to be repeated until the desired color is obtained.

DECORATING ZINC.

A beautiful and permanent dark or light green coating, resembling enamel, can be applied to all kinds of zinc articles, especially those made of sheet zinc, in the following manner: Fifty parts of hyposulphite of soda are dissolved in 500 of boiling water, and the solution poured at once, in a fine stream, into 25 parts of strong sulphuric acid. The milk of sulphur that separates will soon ball together in lumps and settle. The hot liquid containing sulphate of soda and sulphurous acid is decanted, and the cleansed zinc put in it. In a short time it will acquire a very brilliant, light green coating of sulphide, and only needs to be washed and dried. By exposing it repeatedly and for a longer time to this hot bath, the coating grows thicker and the color darker and more brilliant. The temperature must not fall below 145 degrees Fahr.; when it does it should be heated up to 190 degrees Fahr., to obtain a fine and brilliant deposit.

By dipping these articles in dilute hydrochloric acid, 1 of acid to 3 of water, sulphuretted hydrogen is evolved, and this enamel-like coating loses its lustre and gets lighter in color. Aqueous solutions of aniline colors have little effect upon this dull surface, and none on the gray brilliant coating.

The effect of marbling can be obtained by moistening the gray zinc and applying hydrochloric acid in spots with a sponge, then rinsing it off, and while still wet flowing over it an acidified solution of sulphate of copper, which produces the appearance of black marble. As the zinc has generally a dull surface it must receive a coat of copal varnish. If 15 grammes of chrome alum and 15 more of hyposulphite of soda be added to the above solution, the article will have a brownish color. The above can all be applied to articles made of cost-iron.

DELALOT'S ALLOY.

Delalot's alloy is composed of

2 parts Manganese,
18 parts Zinc,
1 part Phosphate of Lime,
80 parts Fine Copper.

The copper is first melted and then the manganese is gradually added, and after its complete dissolution the phosphate of lime is added. The scoria is removed and the zinc is added about ten minutes before casting. The fusion from the manganese will be facilitated by the addition of 1 part charcoal, ½ part borax and ½ calcium fluoride.

DELTA METAL.

Delta metal is an alloy of zinc, iron and copper, to which, during fusion, phosphorus is added, and then, according to the use it is to be put, further additions of tin, lead and manganese. This metal has the color of a gold-silver alloy, and can be worked either hot or cold. You cannot weld it, and it is soldered with difficulty. It does not rust. A common composition of this metal is as follows: Copper, 55 82-100 per cent.; lead, 76-100 per cent.; manganese, 1 38-100 per cent.; iron, 76-100 per cent.; nickel, 6-100 per cent.; zinc, 41 41-100 per cent.

DISCOVERING LEAD IN TIN.

To discover lead in tin, a small bit of tin is detached and put into a watch glass, with a drop of nitric acid and two or three drops of water; the glass is then gently heated over a flame, and when the solution is complete a few drops of water and a concentrated solution of iodine of potassium are added, when, if lead is present, a yellow precipitate will be the result.

DISTINGUISHING CAST-IRON, STEEL AND WROUGHT IRON.

Brighten the surface of the article to be tested by filing, and apply a drop of nitric acid. Allow the acid to work for a few minutes, then wipe same off and rinse with water. If the metal be wrought iron, a dead white or ash-gray spot can be seen. If cast-iron, a deep black one. If steel, a brownish-black one.

ENAMELING CAST-IRON.

A new process for enameling cast-iron objects, in which the principle is adopted that the enamel will take better on white than on gray iron, as the latter contains a quantity of free carbon (graphite). Sulphur is used in casting which will unite and form sulphuret of carbon, and the iron is covered with a skin of white iron where exposed to the action of the sulphur. Ready-made objects are painted over with sulphuric acid of 60 degrees Fahr., and then heated, by which means the acid in the pores acts on the graphite in a similar manner.

ENAMELING CASTINGS.

The formula consists in treating the castings with dilute hydrochloric acid, which dissolves a little of the metal, and leaves a skin of homogeneous graphite holding well to the iron. The iron is then washed in a receiver with hot or cold water, or cooked in steam, so as to remove completely the iron chloride that has been formed. Finally, the piece is allowed to dry in the empty receiver, and a solution of India rubber or gutta percha, in essence of petroleum, is injected, and the solvent, afterwards evaporated, leaves a hard and solid enamel on the surface of the iron work. Another plan is to keep the chloride of iron on the metal instead of washing it off, and to plunge the piece into a bath of soda silicate and borate. Thus is formed a silico-borate of iron, very hard and brilliant, which fills the pores of the metal skin. As for the chlorine disengaged, it continues with the soda to form sodium chloride, which remains in the pickle.

ENAMELING IRONWARE WITH PORCELAIN.

Ironware is enameled with porcelain by first cleaning the surface free from moulding sand, then heating the article in an oven to a low red in the dark, or what is called a black heat, to slightly oxidize the surface and free it from grease. Then brush the powdered enamel mixed with water, and dry quickly. Then bake with a red heat. For the second, or finishing coat, brush on the glazed coat and treat as the first. For the first coat make a mixture of 66 parts calcined flint ground to a powder, 34 parts borax. Melt these together and pulverize, then add 12 parts potter's clay. Mix the whole with water to the consistency of paint, and apply. For the glaze coat take 15 parts borax, 73 parts powdered glass, 12 parts soda. Mix and melt, then pulverize and apply with water. Bake at a red heat.

ENAMEL—TEST FOR.

To test the enamel of ordinary kitchen utensils for the presence of lead, apply a drop of concentrated nitric acid to the enamel of the vessel, first carefully cleaning same, and evaporate it until dry, with a moderate heat. Then wet the place, subject it to the action of the acid with a drop of sodium iodide, and if there is lead present a yellow iodide of lead will be formed.

ENGLISH SILVER SOAP.

This polish is made by the dissolution, in 2 parts of water (soft), of 2 parts of Castile soap. The resultant paste is stirred into 6 parts of fine whiting, poured into molds and cooled. If it is desired that this soap should have a rose tinge, substitute for the whiting 2 parts (finest quality) white tripoli, 1 part jewelers' rouge and 3 parts pulverized chalk. Perfume the soap before putting it into the molds with a drop or two of oil of Lavender, which gives it a very dainty odor.

ENGLISH STERLING METAL.

English sterling metal is a copper-zinc alloy composed of

66 2-10 parts Copper,
33 1-10 parts Zinc,
7-10 parts Iron.

ETCHING LIQUID FOR STEEL.

Mix 1 ounce sulphate of copper, ½ ounce of alum, and ½ teaspoonful of salt reduced to powder, with 1 gill of vinegar and 20 drops of nitric acid. This liquid may be used for either eating deeply into the metal or for imparting a beautiful frosted appearance to the surface, according to the time it is allowed to act. Cover the parts you wish to protect from its influence with beeswax, tallow or some other similar substance.

ETCHING NAMES ON STEEL.

With equal quantities of copper sulphate (blue vitriol), sodium chloride (common salt), well-powdered and mixed together, names or other marks can be etched on steel. The wax process must be used, although soap will answer, or any other substance not coated upon by acids. Spread the beeswax or soap in a thin, even coating, over the article to be etched, and with a sharp-pointed awl, write or draw the design upon the wax-covered surface. Every line must be cut cleanly, and every particle of the coating removed, otherwise a break will appear in the etched line. When the drawing has been made satisfactory, put a "tinker's dam" around the wax-covered spot; this is done by rolling out a piece of putty into a long, thin roll, bend it around the wax-covered spot and press it lightly down, thus making a little reservoir to hold the acid or other corroding substance. Mix up the salt and sulphate of copper, fill inside the dam and moisten with water to hasten their action. When satisfied that the etching is deep enough, or tired of waiting for it to work, wash off the corroding mixture and scrape off the wax, or dissolve it away with turpentine, alcohol or naphtha. If the etching is not deep enough, an ink roller, such as is used on printing presses, may be passed over the surface, a coating of ink put on. This will prevent any acid action upon the surface thus protected, and the solution may be reapplied until the etching is sufficiently deep. If successive etchings are necessary, the plate should be rinsed and warmed after each removal of the corroding solution, and more ink applied before another lot of fresh corroder is put to work.

In regular work, where large numbers of zinc etchings are made, "dragon's blood" is used to protect the surface instead of printer's ink, but for occasional work ink is good enough. Nitric and sulphuric acids may be used for etching, and the effect of the composition described at the beginning of this article depends upon the chlorine and sulphuric acid set free by the combination of the two salts.

ETCHING ON GLASS.

For etching on glass, prepare the glass by warming it and rubbing white wax over it until the surface is covered thinly. Trace the design through the wax with a pointed instrument. Pour on liquid fluoric acid and leave to act upon the glass; this will make a clean, transparent cut. To produce opaque lines, like ground glass or frosted work, place the fluoric acid in a lead utensil and place in hot sand, or in some way warm the acid without melting the lead pan. Place the prepared glass over the pan, and the fumes from the acid will act upon the glass. This should be done out of doors or in some place where the fumes will not be inhaled. A simple method of the process is to wet the prepared glass with sulphuric acid and then sprinkle on finely powdered flour spar (Fluoride of calcium), by which hydrofluoric acid is set free and attacks the glass.

ETCHING ON STEEL.

The process is similar to that used by engravers. Acid is spread over the part to be etched, then the figures or name is cut on with a needle-point, and the acid and cold bath finishes the work.

FASTENING ASBESTOS TO IRON.

To fasten asbestos to iron use billsticker's paste; prepared asbestos, which comes in cans, will adhere of itself when it dries.

FASTENING KNIFE AND FORK HANDLES.

A material for fastening knives or forks into their handles when they have become loosened by use, is a much-needed article. The best cement for this purpose consists of 1 pound of colophony (purchasable at the druggist's), and 8 ounces of sulphur, which are to be melted together, and either kept in bars or reduced to a powder. One part of the powder is to be mixed with half a part of iron filings, fine sand, or brickdust, and the cavity of the handle is then to be filled with this mixture. The stem of the knife or fork is then to be heated and inserted into the cavity, and when cold it will be found fixed in its place with great tenacity.

FASTENING LEATHER TO IRON.

To fasten leather to iron, digest one part of crushed nut-galls for six hours with eight of distilled water, and strain the mass. Soak glue in its own weight of water for twenty-four hours and then dissolve it. The warm infusion of galls is spread upon the leather and the glue solution on the roughened surface of the warm metal, the moist leather is pressed upon it and, when dry, it adheres so firmly that it cannot be removed without tearing.

FASTENING PAPER LABELS TO IRON.

The place where the label is to be put is rubbed with half an onion. The label is then stuck on with gum, glue or paste. The firm adherence of the vegetable mucilage of the onion to the iron and its combination with the paste on the paper prevents any cracking off. This will also stand heat.

FASTENING ROOF.

How to fasten a tin roof that has worked loose: Cut

tin strips about 1 inch long by ½ inch in width, and use ¾ inch screws. Lay the strip of tin close to the seam; after scraping the paint off sufficiently, punch a hole through one end, put in a screw, turn the tin over the head and solder well.

FASTENING TIN DOWN.

In fastening tin down which has become loose, use No. 7 screws, ¾ inch. Take a small piece of tin ⅝ of an inch wide by 1⅛ inch long, punch a hole in one end, leaving room to cover the screw head and solder well. Use resin and hot copper to take the paint off in good shape by brushing with a broom while hot. The tin holds the screw better than solder alone.

FERRIC CHLORIDE.

Ferric chloride is made by the addition of chlorine water to a solution of ferrous chloride. I can also be made by the dissolution of ferric oxide in hydra-chloric acid. If placed in water, it dissolves into a yellow fluid.

FERRIC OXIDE.

For polishing purposes Ferric oxide is used both in a natural and in a prepared state. The natural ferric oxide, such as specular and red iron ores, hematite, etc., should be ground fine and elutriated. A common form of ferric oxide is found in the polishing agent variously known as crocus, colcothar, jewelers' rouge (or red) or caput mortuum, which is obtained by heating ferric sulphate in a preparation of fuming sulphuric acid.

FERRIC SULPHATE.

Ferric sulphate is made by heating 5 parts of ferrous sulphate with 1 part of sulphuric acid and 15 parts of water, and adding to the boiling solution nitric acid in small quantities until the color of the fluid changes from black to a brownish-yellow. When evaporated, it yields a pale-yellow crystalline mass which, on the compounding with sulphuric acid, gives anhydrous ferric sulphate.

FERRO-MANGANESE.

Ferro-manganese is composed of

75 parts Manganese,
75 parts Iron.

FERROUS CHLORIDE.

Ferrous chloride is made by the dissolution of iron in hydro-chloric acid. After the solution is evaporated pale-green crystals are secured, which oxidize in the air and which easily dissolve in spirit of wine.

FERROUS SULPHATE.

Ferrous sulphate, otherwise known as green vitriol, or copperas, is made by the dissolution of iron filings in dilute sulphuric acid. When the solution is boiling hot it is filtered and the filtered product is mixed with spirit of wine, upon which the ferrous sulphate will separate as a fine, white, crystalline meal, which is washed with spirit of wine and rapidly dried between blotting papers.

FILING CAST-IRON, BRONZE OR BRASS.

In filing large surfaces of cast-iron, bronze or brass, a file with keen cutting teeth is required; use a new file on such surfaces. On narrow surfaces a file that is partly worn can be used with about as good effect as a new file. When a file is so-called worn out on brass or soft metal, it is in pretty good condition to be used on steel or iron. Many mechanics prefer such files to new ones.

FIRE BRICK.

A good lining for stoves may be made by pulverizing old brick, or any fire brick, and mixing with this sufficient clay to make it plastic. Before making a coal fire dry out the water. The coal fire will bake and make a solid fire brick lining of your plastic back.

FIRE EXTINGUISHER.

Bicarbonate of ammonia and sulphate of soda in strong solution is the best compound to put in bottles for hand-grenades to extinguish fire.

FLUX FOR HARD SOLDERS.

The best flux for hard solders is a soldering fluid consisting of hydrochloric acid (spirit of salt), saturated with zinc. To prepare this flux put ½ pint of muriatic acid (also called spirits of salts and hydrochloric acid) into a glass, and add small pieces of clean zinc, which will be dissolved by the acid. Let it stand for several hours, till the acid has ceased to act; then add a small quantity of water, say a wineglassful, when boiling will recommence. Let it stand undisturbed for a few hours, and again add a small quantity of water. Continue this until the quantity of water added equals that of the acid (½ pint). When all action has ceased, add 1 ounce of sal-ammoniac; let it stand twelve hours, then decant the clear liquid into a bottle, which should be kept well fastened when not in use. Throw away the sediment, and add a little sal-ammoniac.

FROSTING BRASS.

To frost brass and give it a decorative finish, boil the article in potash, rinse in water, plunge in nitric acid, wash again, then dry in hot sawdust, and give the still hot metal a coat of varnish.

FROSTING TINPLATES.

This is done by heating the tinplate until rather too hot to hold; then dip in a mixture of hydrochloric acid, 1; nitric acid, 1; water, 4. Rinse, dry in hot sawdust (which must be from non-resinous wood), and lacquer—the plate being still hot enough to do everything at one operation, as it were.

FURNACE LINING.

A good compound for lining furnaces is made of 10 parts of lime and 90 parts of ganister. The lime is first burned and slaked, and the addition of the ganister is made twelve hours afterward. The addition of enough water for the required consistency is then made and the whole intimately mixed. Line the furnace with the compound and dry by making a moderate fire in the furnace.

GALVANIZING CAST-IRON.

Thoroughly clean the pieces by tumbling, heat them and plunge while hot into the following liquid: Ten pounds hydrochloric acid and sufficient sheet zinc to make a saturated solution. In making this solution, when the evolution of gas has ceased, add muriatic, or, preferably, sulphate of ammonia, 1 pound, and let it stand still dissolved. The castings should be so hot that when dipped in this solution and instantly removed, they will immediately dry, leaving the surface crystallized. Next plunge them while hot, but perfectly dry, in a bath of melted zinc, previously skimming the oxide on the surface away, and throwing thereon a small amount of powdered sal-ammoniac.

Another method, given more in detail, and, therefore, more useful, is as follows:

The castings are first to be cleaned and scoured by immersion in a bath of water acidulated with sulphuric acid. The strength of acid required for this purpose will depend somewhat on the nature of the casting and the amount of scale to be removed. It is sufficient for us to say, however, in this connection, that the surface of the casting must be made perfectly clean in order to insure satisfactory results in the subsequent processes. They may be scoured with sand and water or scraped with a tool in order to make sure that every portion of the surface has become clean. After the parts have thus been cleaned they are thrown into cold water in order to prevent oxidation. Pure zinc, covered with a thick layer of sal-ammoniac, is then melted in a bath and the iron is dipped in the preparation. In removing the pieces they are raised slowly to allow of draining, and are then thrown into cold water. The latter is done in order to keep the surface bright. Where the parts are very large it is necessary to heat them somewhat before plunging them into the molten bath of zinc, as otherwise the presence of so large a body of cold metal would chill the zinc and prevent the formation of a satisfactory coating. The object of the coat of sal-ammoniac above the melted zinc is to prevent the waste of zinc and also to act as a flux to the pieces passing through it into the metal. In some cases the sal-ammoniac is mixed with earthy matter or sand, in order to lessen the volatilization of the sal-ammoniac, which becomes quite fluid. In order to give a crystalline appearance to the surface coated by the zinc, sometimes a light coating of tin is given to the article.

GALVANIZING WITH GOLD.

To galvanize with gold, dissolve a little gold in a mixture of muriatic acid and aqua fortis, and add to it 2 parts of alcohol. Copper immersed in this solution for half an hour will be completely galvanized.

GERMAN BRITANNIA METAL.

German Britannia metal is composed of

4 parts Copper,
24 parts Ammonia,
72 parts Tin,
or
5 parts Zinc,
2 parts Copper,
9 parts Antimony,
84 parts Tin,
or
6 parts Zinc,
10 parts Copper,
64 parts Antimony,
20 parts Tin.

GILDING—LIGHT—TEST FOR.

To discover if any metal has a thin gold coating or whether its appearance is due to a gilding lacquer, clean a portion of the article which you desire tested with either ether or alcohol and dissolve same in nitric acid free from any trace of chlorine. If the article is gilded, the layer of the gold floats in or upon the solution. When a removal of the varnish coatings cannot be brought about by ether or alcohol, treatment by chloroform is required. To make sure of the presence of gold the following test will be found useful: Completely dissolve the article to be tested in nitric acid, dilute resultant solution with water, filter, preferably with a small filter, wash out, dry and glow. The glowed residue is treated with the aid of heat, with a small portion of aqua regia poured off or filtered, as necessity requires, and the filtrate evaporated until dry, at a moderate heat. If there is gold in the article a slight lustrous separation of some will be seen on the edges of the vessel. Mix the residue from evaporation with from 12-100 to 18-100 cubic inches of water, and divide the resultant solution into three portions, which are to be used in the following tests:

(1) Add a drop of concentrated solution of protochloride; if there is any gold in the mixture there is a resultant dark-brown separation.

(2) Add to mixture a drop of solution of ferrous sulphate; the presence of gold gives a brownish or bluish separation.

(3) Add oxygenated water; the pressure of gold will give a blue separation.

(4) To determine whether gold or alloys have been used for gilding, a solution of chloride of copper will be found efficacious. If the gilding be imitation gold, a touch of the solution gives a black mark, the copper separating out through the zinc in the yellow metal—there is no such discoloration if the metal be pure. Another test is a solution of nitrate of silver, or chloride of gold. The first of these will give a gray or black spot and the second a brown spot, if the gilding be imitation gold, but neither have any effect on the genuine metal.

GLAZING METALS.

A mixture of 20 parts of carbonate of soda, 11 of boracic acid, and 125 of broken (flint) glass and melted, and the mass poured out on a stone or plate of metal. When cold it is pulverized and mixed with a silicate of soda (water glass) solution of 50 degrees Fahr. The metal is covered with this paste and then heated until it melts. This enamel is said to adhere well to iron and steel.

GLUING CLOTH TO TIN.

To fix a metallic to a soft substance requires a tough substance, not a varnish, nor yet a glue, but India-rubber cement. Warm the metal and rub over with the cement, and when yet hot, apply the cloth and press with a hot flatiron.

GLUING LABELS ON TIN BOXES.

Labels can be glued on tin boxes, etc., exposed to moisture, by the following process, and they will not come off, even if dipped or allowed to remain in water.

The white of an egg should be mixed with half as much water, or the dessicated albumen of commerce dissolved in two or three times its weight in water. Apply with a brush to the surfaces to be united, then iron with a very hot flatiron. Several layers of paper and glue thus treated will render any box or anything of the kind impermeable to water.

GLUING LEATHER TO IRON.

To glue leather to iron, paint the iron with some kind of lead color, say that and lampblack; when dry cement with a cement made as follows: Take the best glue, soak it in cold water till soft, then dissolve in vinegar with a moderate heat, then add one-third of its bulk of pure turpentine, thoroughly mix, and by means of the vinegar make it of the proper consistency to be spread with a brush, and apply it while hot; draw the leather on quickly and press it tightly in place. If a pulley, draw the leather around as tightly as possible, lap and clamp.

GOLD BEATING.

To beat gold, put same into a stone crucible, melt and pour it into a mold, thus giving it a right width for rolling. Run it through rollers whose pressure is such that a bar of gold 1 inch thick, say, and about 3 inches long, after being rolled several times, becomes a strip about 14 yards long and as thick as a hair. These strips are to be cut into inch squares, which are put into a receptacle technically known as a "cutch," made of 180 skins, 3½ inches square. Vellum is a good substance to use for these skins. Alternate the gold squares and the pieces of skin until the "cutch" is filled up. Then beat the cutch for about a quarter of an hour with a 16-lb hammer, take out the gold, divide it into quarters with a skewer and put them in a shoder. The skins in a shoder come from the bum-gut of an ox, each animal furnishing but two skins. These shoder skins are 4 inches square and the gold squares are alternated in them the same as they were in the cutch. After beating them for about one and a half hours, with a 10-lb. hammer, they are taken out and quartered with a small piece of reed. Then put them in a mold until the latter is filled and beat with a 7-lb. hammer for three or four hours. The leaf is then ready for trimming. It will be observed that with each successive beating the length of time becomes longer and the size of the hammer smaller.

GOLD BRONZE.

Gold bronze powder, such as is used for decorating furniture, tinware, etc., is composed of bisulphate of tin. It may be mixed with copal varnish for application.

GOLD BRONZING FOR IRON.

A superior gold bronze iron is obtained by the dissolution of 3 ounces of finely powdered shellac in 1¾ pints of spirits of wine. This varnish is to be filtered through linen and with the filtrate you must triturate enough Dutch gold to give is a lustrous appearance. Brush the iron previously polished and heated over with vinegar, and apply the color with a brush. After it is dry coat the article with a mixture of copal and amber lacquer.

GOLD-COLORED SURFACE ON BRASS.

A gold-colored surface on brass may be produced with a liquid prepared by boiling together for about fifteen minutes 4 parts of caustic soda, 4 parts of milk sugar, and 100 parts of water, to which 4 parts of a concentrated solution of sulphate of copper should then be added with constant stirring. The mixture is then cooled to 67 degrees Fahr., and the well-cleansed articles are immersed in it for a short time, when the gold color will appear. A longer immersion results in the formation of a bluish green tint, and a still more prolonged action causes the formation of iridescent colors.

GOLD—GENUINE—TEST FOR.

To test gold for its genuineness, dissolve in chlorine water and the resultant solution will possess a slightly yellowing color.

GOLD SALT.

Gold salt is prepared by dissolution of 8 parts of gold in aqua regia. Two parts of common salt are added and the solution evaporated to dryness. A second method consists in the dissolution of 1 part gold in a mixture of 1 part of nitric acid and 4 parts of hydro-chloric acid.

GOLD STAINS FOR BRASS.

To give gold stains to brass the articles are to be immersed in a compound of

5½ drachms damp Carbonate of Copper,
3 drachms Caustic Soda,
2 ounces Water.

It will be only a few minutes before the shades of

color make their appearance, and by watching same the appearance of the exact shade can be observed. When this is obtained the article is to be rinsed in water and dried in fine, soft dust.

GOLD TO PURIFY.

To purify gold, make a thorough mixture of

1 part Vitriol (green),
1 part Sea Salt,
1 part Alum,
3 parts Brickdust.

Form this compound into a paste by the addition of a little wine vinegar, and place the gold in the center of it.

GOLD WARE—TEST FOR.

A good method for the testing of gold ware is presented by the touchstone, which is a kind of black, Silesian basalt. When you draw a piece of gold across its surface a gold streak is left, which is unaffected by nitric acid moistening and which differs from streaks left by brass and other base alloys, which rapidly dissolve.

GRAY COATING ON ZINC.

To obtain a gray coating on zinc precipitate arsenic in a heated bath of 8 46-100 drachms sodium pyro-phosphate in 8 2-100 ounces arsenious and 1¾ drachms of 98 per cent. potassium cyanide to 1 quart of water. Use a current strong enough so that a strongly perceptible development of hydrogen ensues.

For anodes use either carbon plates or platinum sheets.

GRAY COLOR FOR IRON AND STEEL.

To give iron and steel a gray color first polish the article and then coat it with a mixture of 2 parts of sulphuric acid, a drop or two of acetic acid and 8 parts of butter antimony.

GREEN COATING FOR ZINC.

To give zinc a dark or light green coating dissolve

50 parts hydro-sulphite of sodium in 500 parts of boiling water and immediately pour the solution into 25 parts of sulphuric acid. This will cause the milk and sulphur to separate and then ball together in lumps and settle. The hot liquid containing sulphurous acid and sulphate of sodium is decanted, and in it the zinc, first cleansed, is placed. It will not be long before it will acquire a brilliant light-green coating, which only needs to be washed and dried. The longer the exposure of the zinc to this hot bath, the thicker the coating and the darker and more brilliant the color. It is essential, in order to insure a fine and brilliant deposit, that the temperature should not be allowed to fall below 145 degrees Fahrenheit. Dip the articles thus treated in hydro-chloric acid; dilute 1 part of acid to 3 of water and there is a consequent evaporation of sulphureted hydrogen, and this enamel-like coating loses its lustre and becomes lighter in color. This dull surface is not affected by the aqueous solutions of aniline colors. If you desire a brownish color for your article add 15 parts of chrome alum and 15 more of the hypo-sulphite to the above solution.

GUM COPAL.

Copal varnish is one of the very finest varnishes for japanning purposes. It can be dissolved by linseed oil, rendered dry by adding some quicklime at a heat somewhat less than will boil or decompose the oil by it.

This solution, with the addition of a little turpentine, forms a very transparent varnish, which, when properly applied and slowly dried, is very hard and durable. This varnish is applied to snuff boxes, tea boards and other utensils. It also preserves paintings and renders their surfaces capable of reflecting light more uniformly.

If powdered copal be mixed in a mortar with camphor it softens and becomes a coherent mass, and if camphor be added to alcohol it becomes an excellent solvent of copal by adding the copal well ground, and employing a tolerable degree of heat, having the vessel well corked, which must have a long neck for the allowance of expansion, and the vessel must only be about one-fourth filled with the mixture. Copal can also be incorporated with turpentine, with one part powdered copal to twelve parts pure turpentine, subjected to the heat of a sand-bath for several days in a long-necked mattress, shaking it frequently.

Copal is a good varnish for metals, such as tin; the varnish must be dried in an oven, each coat, and it can be colored with some substances, but alcohol varnish will mix with any color.

GUN METAL.

Copper, 18 parts; tin, 2 parts. Melt.

HAND FIRE GRENADES—SOLUTION FOR.

Bicarbonate of ammonia and sulphate of soda in strong solution for hand grenades to extinguish fire. This compound will keep indefinitely without losing its active properties if the bottle is kept well corked.

HARDENING CAST-IRON.

To harden cast-iron mix 2 ounces nitric acid and 2 pounds concentrated sulphuric acid with 2½ gallons of water. The article is to be plunged into this mixture when at a cherry red heat.

HARDENING COMPOUND FOR STEEL.

A compound for hardening steel consists of 3 parts of yellow prussiate of potash pulverized, 1 part pulverized borax, 1 part pulverized saltpetre and ½ part sugar of lead, all intimately mixed. The steel to be hardened is heated to a red heat and is then taken from the fire and this powder scattered over it. The steel is then replaced in the fire and after being brought to the requisite heat is cooled in cold rain water.

HARDENING COMPOUND FOR STEEL AND WROUGHT IRON.

A good hardening compound for steel and wrought iron consists of the following parts, all pulverized and mixed intimately, viz.: One part each of saltpetre and calcined cow's hoofs and yellow prussiate of potash, 1-30 aloes, 1-30 gum-arabic and ½ common salt. The compound is to be scattered upon the wrought iron at a white heat, and steel at a red heat, and thoroughly burnt in.

HARDENING COPPER.

To harden copper melt same with 1 to 6 per cent. of black oxide of manganese in a crucible. This is to be stirred thoroughly and the scum removed before it is poured out. The same method is to be used in preparing brass, a small quantity of zinc being added to the melted copper and oxide of manganese.

HARDENING MIXTURE FOR IRON.

A hardening mixture for iron consists of

1	lb.	Yellow Prussiate of Potash,
½	pt.	Hydro-chloric Acid.
2	oz.	Charcoal,
2½	lbs.	Bonedust,
2	lbs.	Rock Salt.

The red-hot iron is plunged into this mixture twice, being heated between the two times, and then, while yet hot, is quenched in cold water. These proportions may vary slightly, and at times it is well to add a little lime.

HARDENING SOFT IRON.

To harden soft iron wet it with water and scatter over its surface powdered yellow prussiate of potash. Then heat to a cherry red heat, which causes the potash to melt and coat the surface of the soft iron. Then immerse quickly in cold water and repeat the operation. A white heat must not be used, as this would not harden but oxidize the iron. Care must be used not to use red prussiate of potash instead of the yellow. It will not answer.

HARDENING STEEL PIANO-WIRE.

To harden steel piano-wire first heat it red-hot and

then cool. Next plunge same in a bath composed of

21 parts Tin,
26 parts Antimony,
12 parts Zinc,
1 part Bismuth,
40 parts Lead.

This bath should be heated above its melting point and the wire should stay in it until it has acquired the temperature of the bath. The time which this takes varies directly with the thickness of the wire.

HARDENING TOOLS.

In order to harden tools without making them warp or having their interior become too hard and brittle, the following compound will be found desirable:

500 parts Peruvian Bark,
25 parts Common Salt,
15 parts Yellow Prussiate of Potash,
15 parts Saltpetre,
50 parts Hartshorn Shavings,
100 parts Black Soap.

Spread the soap in a layer 39-100 of an inch deep, then scatter on it the pulverized mixture of the other substances and knead the paste thus formed. Continue this kneading until the mass is formed into a stick about 2 inches in diameter. Allow this compound to dry for twenty-four hours before using, then care must be taken to heat the cast-steel article only to dark red.

Then the portions to be hardened are coated with the compound and cooled off. When this is done the interior as well as the portions not coated remain soft and tough, while the coated portions become hard as glass. To find the degree cast-steel should be heated for this, it is perhaps well to experiment with a round steel wire, about ½ inch thick.

HARDENING ZINC.

To harden zinc bring into the melted metal from 1 76-100 to 3 52-100 ounces of sal-ammoniac per pound.

IMPROVING THE COLOR AFTER BRASS HAS BEEN JOINED WITH WHITE SOLDER.

If brass has been joined with white solder the difference of color invites attention to the part where the junction has been effected. This may be obviated, it is said, by applying a saturated solution of sulphate of copper to the solder. If the place is then touched with a steel or iron wire it becomes coppered, and the coating of copper increases in thickness as the operation is repeated. To give the required yellow color, one part of saturated solution of sulphate of zinc is added to two parts of sulphate of copper. This mixture is applied to the coppered spot. and is rubbed in with a rod of zinc. The color can be further improved by using a gilding powder and by polishing.

INK—CARMINE.

To make red or carmine ink for bookkeeping purposes: Take 12 grains of carmine, add 3 ounces of aqua ammonia and heat gently, without boiling, for seven or eight minutes; then add 18 grains of gum arabic, stirring constantly. Keep well corked.

INK—COPYING.

Ink for copying without a press: A regular copying outfit is desirable and most satisfactory for this purpose, but not absolutely essential. Mixing a little glycerine into the ink with which the letter is written will enable the letter to be copied by laying it face downward on tissue paper and rubbing with the hand over the back of the letter. Perhaps a more satisfactory way is to prepare a special ink for this purpose, as follows: Heat one ounce extract of logwood, broken coarsely, and one drachm of carbonate of soda (crystallized) in a porcelain vessel containing 8 ounces of rain water until the solution is of a deep red color; remove from the fire and stir in 1 ounce of glycerine, 15 grains of neutral chromate of potash, dissolved in a little water, and two drachms of a mucilaginous solution of finely pulverized gum arabic. The impression of the letter is taken on thin moistened copying paper, at the back of which is placed a sheet of writing paper.

INK FOR MARKING TINWARE.

A good ink for marking tinware is composed of the following: Reduce asphalt or black varnish with turpentine to the desired consistency and keep it in a corked bottle. When you use it shake the bottle and hold varnish side up after withdrawing the cork.

Another ink can be made by reducing shellac varnish with alcohol and adding a sufficient quantity of lampblack. This forms a jet black, lusterless ink, which is insoluble in water, but can be removed by a drop of alcohol. For marking on tin plates, mix together, without the use of heat, 1 part of pine soot with 60 parts of solution of nitrate of copper in water.

INK FOR RUBBER STAMPS.

Rubber stamps are now in universal use for business purposes, and are used with inks of various colors. These inks anyone may make for himself. They are usually prepared by dissolving aniline colors in water and adding glycerine. An excellent blue rubber stamp ink is made of three parts aniline blue 1 B., 10 parts distilled water, 10 parts pyroligneous acid, 10 parts alcohol, 70 parts glycerine. Rub the blue down with water, add the glycerine gradually, and when the solution is effected add the other ingredients. Other colors can be substituted for blue as follows: Three parts methyl violet; 2 parts diamond juchsin I.; 4 parts methyl green; yellowing, 5 parts Vesuvian B. (brown); 4 parts nigrosin W. (blue-black); omit the pyroligneous acid and use 3 parts eosin BBN for bright red.

INK FOR STENCIL MARKING.

A fine ink for stencil marking is made as follows: Sulphate of manganese, 2 parts; lampblack, 1 part; sugar, 4 parts; all in fine powder and triturated to a paste with a little water.

INK FOR WRITING ON STEEL.

To make ink for writing on steel, tinplate or sheet zinc, mix 1 ounce of powdered sulphate of copper, and ½ ounce powdered sal-ammoniac, with 2 ounces of diluted acetic acid, adding lampblack or vermillion.

INK FOR WRITING ON TIN.

An ink for writing on tin is made by the dissolution of 1 part copper in 10 parts nitric acid, to which solution 10 parts of water is added. The tin should be cleaned with dry whiting, and the writing should be done with a quill.

INK FOR WRITING ON ZINC.

To write on zinc first clean the surface of the zinc by rubbing with a sponge which has been plunged in dilute hydro-chloric acid and fine sand. Next dissolve 1 ounce and 4 drachms of sal-ammoniac and 1 ounce and 4 drachms of crystallized verdigris in a pint of warm water. Filter the solution after it has cooled and keep it in tightly corked bottles. After the zinc has been written on by this compound it should be allowed to remain in water for a few hours, and then dried and used without varnish. The writing should be (preferably) done with a quill. Should the zinc look greasy or should the writing run together the surface should be cleaned with a rag dipped in chalk.

INSULATING COVERING FOR STEAM PIPES.

Insulating coverings for steam pipes is made by boiling together

1 lb. Rye Flour,
1 lb. Rice Flour,
1 lb. Treacle,
1 lb. Cow's Hair,
with
150 qts. Water.

to which mass 80 lbs. of infusorial earth is gradually stirred. This compound should be applied in several layers to the slightly warmed pipes, so that a layer a little more than ½ inch in thickness is formed.

(2) Another covering for steam pipes is made from asbestos pulp, cork waste and felt, filled into a casting surrounding the pipes.

(3) Another compound for the insulation of steam pipes consists of

250 parts Pulverized Clay,
300 parts Fine Ashes from Boiler Flues,
100 parts Finely Ground Limestone,
350 parts Finely Ground Coal.

These are to be intimately mixed with

600 parts Water,
10 parts Sulphuric Acid (of 50 degrees Be.)

and after the addition of 15 parts of hogs' bristles the compound is to be made as homogeneous as possible. Heat the article to be covered, and then gradually apply this compound in separate layers of one-half an inch thickness until a thickness of 1½ to 1¾ inches is obtained.

INSULATION FOR ELECTRICAL CONDUITS.

A good insulating material for electrical conduits is made by the mixture of 34 parts finely pulverized resin with 66 parts fine glass or quartz powder. To this compound the addition is to be made of 26 parts of either beeswax, spermaceti or paraffine and 36 parts of either crude or boiled linseed oil. The proportions of the various ingredients should be in accordance with circumstances. If the compound is intended for exposure to the sun, the amount of wax used should be small; while the converse is true should the compound be employed for underground lines. Another insulating material for electrical conduits is made by constantly stirring in a boiler, at a heat between 92 degrees and 212 degrees Fahrenheit,

29 parts Wood Tar,
36 parts Shellac,
32 parts Asbestos,
1 part Mineral Wax.

Should this compound be insufficiently hard, a smaller quantity of wood tar can be used. If a mass of extraordinary hardness is desired, the amount of asbestos used can be decreased and wax can be omitted and about 24 parts of infusorial earth clay, without any traces of iron in it, or ground slate, can be used.

IRON PLATES—CUTTING OUT WITH SULPHURIC ACID.

To cut out iron plates with sulphuric acid, compound together 1 part of acid with 6 of water. Then coat the iron with wax, drawing the required design in same and placing the plate in this compound for several hours, which will cause the parts making the design to drop out. The same process is to be pursued for etching names, ornaments, letters, etc., upon sword-blades.

IRIDESCENT METAL COLORING.

In order to cause the colors of the rainbow to appear upon gilded articles of brass, iron and other metals, as well as any other clean metal surface, make a bath by boiling for a half hour 14½ drachms litharge and 3½ ounces caustic soda with 1 quart of water. The object to be colored, which should have been first thoroughly pickled and cleaned, is to be connected with the wire of the positive pole of a bettery, while, as an anode, a platinum wire is used. If this wire is plunged in the bath without coming in contact with the article the layer at once is colored with a variety of colors, which take their origin from a more or less thick layer of the precipitated oxide of lead. If a piece of stout parchment paper is placed in a vertical position between the articles to be colored and the platinum wire, colors of all possible contrasts may be obtained. The parchment, however, should also be provided with radical segments, or numerous holes.

ISOLIT.

Isolit is the commercial name of a matrix mass for reproducing coins, medals, etc. It is composed of ozokerite in a pure state with the addition of 5 per cent. of sulphur and 7 per cent. of petroleum.

JAPAN—BLACK.

Black japan is made from Naples asphaltum, 50 pounds; dark gum-amime, 8 pounds, use, add linseed oil, 12 gallons; boil; add dark gum amber, 10 pounds, previously fused and boiled with linseed oil, 2 gallons; add the dryers. Used for wood or metal.

(2) Black japan is made: 1. Asphaltum, 3 ounces; boiled oil, 4 quarts; burnt amber, 8 ounces. Mix by heat, and when cooling thin with turpentine. 2. Amber, 12 ounces; asphaltum, 2 ounces; fuse by heat. Add boiled oil, ½ pint; resin, 2 ounces. When cooling add 16 ounces oil of turpentine. Both are used to varnish metals.

JAPANNING—BLACK GROUND FOR.

A good black ground for japanning is prepared by grinding fine ivory black with a sufficient quantity of alcoholic shellac varnish on a stone slab with a muller until perfectly smooth black varnish is obtained. If other colors are required the varnish is mixed and ground with the proper quantity of suitable pigments in a similar manner. The following are good common black grounds:

(1) Asphaltum, 1 pound; balsam of copaiba, 1 pound; oil of turpentine, q. s. The asphaltum is melted over a fire, and the balsam, previously heated, is mixed with it. The mixture is then removed from the fire and mixed with turpentine.

(2) Moisten good lampblack with oil of turpentine, and grind it very fine with a muller on a stone plate. Then add a sufficient quantity of ordinary copal varnish and rub well together.

(3) Asphaltum, 3 ounces; boiled oil, 4 quarts; burnt amber, 8 ounces; oil of turpentine, q. s. Melt the asphaltum, stir in the oil, previously heated, then the umber, and when cooling thin down with the oil of turpentine.

An extra black is prepared from: Amber, 12 oz.; asphaltum, purified, 2 oz.; boiled oil, ½ pint; resin, 2 oz.; oil of turpentine, 16 oz. Fuse the gum and resin and asphaltum, and the hot oil, stir well together, and when cooling add the turpentine. A white ground is prepared from copal varnish and zinc white or starch. From one to six or more coats of varnish are applied to the work of japanning, each coat being hardened in the oven before the next is put on. The last coat in colored work is usually clear varnish.

JAPAN—BLACK GROUNDS FOR.

Black grounds for japans may be made by mixing ivory black with shellac varnish; or for coarse work, lampblack and the top coating of common seed lac varnish. A common black japan may be made by painting a piece of work with drying oil (oil mixed with lead) and putting the work into a stove, not too hot, but of such a degree, gradually raising the heat and keeping it up for a long time, so as not to burn the oil and make it blister. This process makes very fair japan and requires no polishing.

JAPAN GROUNDS—BLUE.

Blue japan grounds may be formed of bright Prussian blue. The color may be mixed with shellac varnish, and brought to a polishing state by five or six coats of varnish of seed lac. The varnish, however, is apt to give a greenish tinge to the blue, as the varnish has a yellowish tinge, and blue and yellow form a green. Whenever a light blue is desired the purest varnish must always be used.

JAPAN GROUNDS—GREEN.

A good green japan ground may be made by mixing Prussian blue with the chromate of lead, or with tumeric, or orpimen (sulphuret of arsenic), or ochre, only the two should be ground together and dissolved in alcohol and applied as a ground, then coated with four or five coats of shellac varnish. A very bright green is made by laying on a ground of Dutch metal, or leaf of gold, and then coating it over with distilled verdigris dissolved in alcohol, then the varnishes on the top. This is a splendid green, brilliant and glowing.

JAPANNING.

The process of japanning upon light iron work, like the frames of oil and gasoline stoves, is simple, but requires an oven constructed on purpose for this kind of work, where any amount of it is to be done. Japan varnish is first applied, and the articles then placed in an oven heated to a temperature of from 250 to 300 degrees. The articles remain in the oven from two to four or more hours, according to the color desired, black and brown requiring the longest baking and being the most durable colors. Light colors require a less degree of heat and not so long time, but are not so durable. For japanning, the ovens are usually made of brick for safety, and heated by an iron flue or stovepipe passing around the room, the fire being on the outside. Some place a heater in a chamber below the drying room, arranged to let the hot air pass up into the drying room. There should be no communication between the hot air chamber and the open fire that could possibly admit the vapor of the varnish to the fire. Steam at high pressure may be used for heating the oven when convenient, and is safer than a stove.

(2) Japanning is the art of covering bodies by grounds of opaque colors in varnish, which may be afterwards decorated by printing or gilding, or left in a plain state. It is also to be looked upon in another sense, as that of ornamenting coaches, snuff-boxes, screens, etc. All surfaces to be japanned must be perfectly clean.

JAPANNING OLD TEA-TRAYS.

First clean them thoroughly with soap and water and a little rotten stone; then dry them by wiping and exposure to the fire. Now, get some good copal varnish, mix with it some bronze powder, and apply with a brush to the denuded parts, after which set the tea-tray in an oven at a heat of 212 or 300 degrees, until the varnish is dry. Two coats will make it equal to new.

JAPAN—ORANGE-COLORED.

Orange-colored japan grounds may be made of yellow mixed with vermilion or carmine, just as a bright or rather inferior color is wanted. The yellow should always be in quantity to make a good full color, and the red added in proportion to the depth of the shade. If there is not a good, full body of yellow, the color will look watery, or bare, as it is technically termed.

JAPAN—PAINTED.

To paint japan work, the colors to be painted are tempered, generally, in oil, which should have at least one-fourth of its weight of gum sandarach, or mastic, dissolved in it, and it should be well diluted with turpentine, that the colors may be laid on thin and evenly. In some instances it does well to put on water colors or grounds of gold, which a skillful hand can do and manage so as to make the work appear as if it was embossed. These water colors are best prepared by means of isinglass size, mixed with honey, or sugar candy. These colors, when laid on, must receive a number of upper coats of varnish.

JAPAN—PURPLE.

Purple japan grounds are made by a mixture of lake and Prussian blue or carmine, or for an inferior color, vermilion. When the ground is laid on and perfectly dried, a fine coat of pure boiled oil is then laid on and perfectly dried, but it is a good method to have a japan not liable to crack. But a better plan is to use this oil in the varnish given, the first coat, after the ground is laid on, and which should contain considerable pure turpentine. In every case where oil is used for any purpose for varnish, it is all the better if turpentine is mixed with it. Turpentine enables oil to mix with either alcohol or water. Alkalies have this property also.

JAPAN—SCARLET.

Ground vermilion may be used for this, but being so glaring it is not beautiful unless covered over with rose-pink or lake, which have a good effect when thus used. For a very bright crimson ground, safflower or Indian lake should be used, always dissolving in the alcohol of which the varnish is made. In place of this lake, carmine may be used, as it is more common. The top coat of varnish must always be of the white seed-lac, and as many coats given as will be thought proper; it is easy to judge of this.

JAPAN—SHEET IRON.

The varnish for black japan consists of pure natural asphaltum with a proportion of gum anime dissolved in linseed oil and thinned with turpentine. In this layers this japan has a rich dark-brown color and only shows a brilliant black in thicker coatings. For fine work, which has to be smoothed and polished, several coats of black are applied in succession, each being separately dried in the stove at a heat which may rise to near 300 degrees Fahr. Body colors consist of a basis of transparent varnish mixed with special mineral paints of the desired color, or with bronze powders. The transparent varnish used by japanners is a copal varnish which contains less drying oil and more turpentine than is contained in the ordinary painters' oil varnish.

JAPAN—TORTOISE SHELL.

This varnish is prepared by taking of good linseed oil 1 gallon, and of umber half a pound, and boiling them together until the oil becomes very brown and thick, when they are strained through a cloth and boiled again until the composition is about the consistency of pitch, when it is fit for use. Having prepared this varnish, clean well the copper or iron plate or vessel that is to be varnished (japanned), and then lay vermilion, mixed with shellac varnish, or with drying oil, diluted with turpentine, very thinly on the places intended to imitate the clean parts of the tortoise shell. When the vermillon is dry brush over the whole with the above umber varnish diluted to a due consistency with turpentine, and when it is set and firm, it must be put into a stove and undergo a strong heat for a long time, even two weeks will not hurt it. This is the ground for these beautiful snuff boxes and tea boards which are so much admired, and these grounds can be decorated with all kinds of paintings that fancy may suggest, and the work is all the better to be finished in an annealing oven.

JAPAN—TRANSPARENT.

Transparent japan may be made of oil of turpentine, 4 ounces; oil of lavender, 3 ounces; camphor, ½ drachm; copal, 1 ounce; dissolve. Used to japan tin, but quick copal varnish is mostly used instead.

JAPAN—YELLOW.

To make yellow japan grounds, dissolve tumeric in spirits of wine, and strain through a cloth, and then mix with pure seed-lac varnish. Saffron will answer for the same purpose in the same way, but the brightest yellow ground is made by a primary coat of pure chrome yellow, and coated successively with the varnish. Dutch pink is used for a kind of cheap yellow japan ground. If a little dragon's blood be added to the varnish for yellow japan, a most beautiful and rich salmon-colored varnish is the result, and by these two mixtures all the shades of flesh-colored japans are produced.

KARAKANE.

Karakane, also called Japanese Bell Metal, is cast in various qualities, among them being the following: 1. Copper (10 parts), tin (2 parts), lead (2 parts). 2. Copper (10 parts), tin (3 parts), lead (2 parts), iron (½ part), zinc (1 part). 3. Copper (10 parts), tin (4 parts), iron (½ part), zinc (1½ parts). 4. Copper (10 parts), tin (2½ parts), lead (1 1-3 parts), zinc (½ part).

KARMASCH'S BRITANNIA METAL.

Karmarsch's Britannia Metal is composed of

1 6-10 parts Bismuth,
1 4-10 parts Zinc,
3 6-10 parts Copper,
5 parts Antimony,
85 parts Tin.

KEEPING MACHINES FROM RUSTING.

To keep machines from rusting: After cleaning well, grease with melted fat in which some camphor has been dissolved, and add to it a sufficient quantity of graphite. After four hours rub with a fine rag.

KEEPING METALS FROM RUSTING.

To keep metals from rusting rub them off perfectly clean and paint them over with the following mixture: Dissolve half an ounce of camphor in a pound of lard, or in that proportion, according to the quantity used, and before it cools enough to be hard, mix in enough black lead to give the whole the color of iron. This should be well and thoroughly applied all over the metal, being careful not to omit any spots, and let it remain over night. The next day rub off clean with rags. If kept dry by the weather, metal treated in this way will keep perfectly free from rust all winter. Olmstead's varnish is made by melting 2 ounces of resin in 1 pound of fresh, sweet lard, melting the resin first and then adding the lard, and then mixing thoroughly. This is applied to the metal, which should be warm, if possible, and perfectly cleaned, and afterward rubbed off. This has been well proved and tested for many years, and it is all that it has been recommended to be. It is particularly well suited for planishes and Russia iron surfaces which a slight rust is apt to injure very seriously.

KEEPING POLISHED EDGES FROM RUSTING.

To keep polished edges from rusting, and still not detract from the appearance of the polished edge, put on a thin film of paraffine.

KEEPING TINWARE BRIGHT.

To keep tinware nice and bright scour it every two or three weeks with finely sifted coal ashes.

KELLER'S BRITANNIA METAL.

Keller's Britannia Metal is composed of

1 8-10	parts	Bismuth,
1	part	Copper,
10 4-10	parts	Antimony,
85 7-10	parts	Tin.

KINDLER—FIRE.

To make a simple and good fire kindler, that will start a coal or wood fire without much trouble: Take 2 quarts of tar and 6 pounds of common resin; melt them; let the mass cool somewhat; then mix it with as much pine sawdust, containing a small portion of charcoal bruised tolerably fine, as can be worked into it. Spread the mixture out upon a board while hot. to the thickness of about an inch, and with an old knife proceed to score it into squares an inch and a half each way, and when cold break up into convenient cakes.

LACQUER—BRASS.

A good lacquer for brass: Tumeric, 1 ounce; saffron, ¼ ounce; annatto, the same quantity; rectified spirits, 1 pint. Digest at gentle heat for several days. Strain the mixture through coarse linen, then put the mixture into a bottle and add 3 ounces of coarsely pulverized seed-lac. Place in a moderate heat and shake occasionally until dissolved.

LACQUER—COFFEE-COLORED.

Lacquer of various tints can be made by putting 4 ounces best gum gamboge into 32 ounces spirits of turpentine, 4 ounces dragon's blood into the same quantity of spirits of turpentine as the gamboge, and 1 ounce annatto into 8 ounces of the same spirits. The three mixtures should be made in different vessels. They should then be kept for about two weeks in a warm place, and as much exposed to the sun as possible. At the end of that time they will be fit for use, and any desired tints may be obtained by making a mixture from them, with such proportions of each liquor as the nature of the color desired will point out.

LACQUER—COLORLESS.

To make a good colorless lacquer, dissolve bleached shellac in pure alcohol, settle and decant. Make the lacquer very thin. The usual lacquer for brass is made of ordinary shellac and alcohol, made very thin, settled and decanted.

LACQUER—ELASTIC.

A very elastic lacquer, perfectly supple, and not liable to peel off, may be made thus: About 120 lbs. of oil varnish are heated in one vessel, and 33 lbs. of quicklime are put into 22 lbs. of water in another. As soon as the lime causes an effervescence, 55 lbs. of india-rubber are added. This mixture is stirred and then poured into the vessel of hot varnish. The whole is instantly stirred so that the ingredients may become completely incorporated. Straining and cooling through the process. When required for use it is thinned with the necessary quantity of varnish, and applied hot or cold to wood, iron, walls, waterproof cloth, paper, or other material.

LACQUER FOR DIPPED BRASS.

A lacquer for dipped brass is composed of the following: Alcohol, proof specific gravity of not less than 95-100ths, 2 gallons; seed-lac, 1 lb.; gum copal, 1 ounce; English saffron, 1 ounce; annatto, 1 ounce.

LACQUER FOR POLISHED BRASS.

The first requisite is to see that the article of polished brass to be lacquered is sufficiently heated to retain the lacquer. This may be done by keeping the surface at a heat above 212 degrees. The lacquer should not be too thick, and may be thinned down with 95 per cent. alcohol, until it appears through the bottle, as a semi-transparent or amber liquid. A few trials with this lacquer and heat applications after lacquering will give success.

LACQUER FOR STEEL.

A lacquer for steel may be made of 10 parts of clear mastic, 5 of camphor, 15 of sandarac, and 5 of elemi gums dissolved in pure alcohol, filtered, and applied cold. This varnish is transparent.

LACQUER FOR TIN.

For a good and cheap lacquer for tinplate: Color lac-varnish with tumeric to impart the color of brass to it, and with annatto to give it the color of copper. Tinplate dipped into molten brass will be coated with it. A deep gold-colored lacquer is made by mixing seed-lac, 3 oz.; tumeric, 1 oz.; dragon's blood, ¼ oz.; alcohol, 1 pint. Digest for a week, frequently shaking, decant and filter.

LACQUER—GOLD.

To a pint of strong alcohol, add as much gamboge as will give it a bright yellow color, then add 2 ounces seed-lac in fine powder, and set it in a warm place until dissolved.

LACQUER—GOLD—FOR METAL GOODS.

A gold lacquer, remarkable both for hardness and for brilliancy of color, is made as follows: A clear solution of shellac is prepared with picric and half per cent. of crystallized boric acid, each separately dissolved in alcohol.

LACQUER—IMITATION JAPANESE.

To make a good imitation of Japanese lacquer, take oil of turpentine, 90 parts, and oil of lavender, 120 parts, and after freeing it from water which may be present by adding a small quantity of calcined calcium chloride, and then carefully pouring off the oil, combine it in a bottle with 2 parts of camphor and

30 parts of copal. Place the bottle for twenty-four hours in hot ashes, shaking it occasionally, and finally filter the contents through a cloth. The filtrate is again allowed to stand for twenty-four hours, when the clear, supernatant fluid is poured off from the sediment.

LEAD CHLORIDE.

Lead chloride is obtained in adding a soluble chloride to a solution of lead salt.

LEAD SULPHATE.

Lead sulphate is a precipitation made by mixing a solution of a lead salt and sulphuric acid.

LECHESNE.

Lechesne is the name of an alloy consisting of

900 parts Copper,
100 parts Nickel,
1¾ parts Aluminum.

It is also made of

600 parts Copper,
400 parts Nickel,
½ part Aluminum.

LETTERING UPON STEEL.

Steel can be written upon or engraved by first cleaning it with oil, and then spreading a coating of melted beeswax upon it. The writing can be done on the beeswax with any sharp instrument, and the lines and marks thus made should be painted with a fine brush dipped in a liquid made of one ounce of nitric acid and one-sixth of an ounce of muriatic acid. When the written lines are filled with this liquid, it should be allowed to remain five minutes, and then the article should be dipped in water and afterwards cleaned.

LINING IRON WITH PORCELAIN.

The white enamel for hollow ware is made of powdered flints, ground with calcined borax, fine clay and a little feldspar. This mixture is made into a paste with water, and brushed over the pots, after they have been thoroughly scoured with dilute sulphuric acid and rinsed clean with water. While still moist, they are dusted over with a glaze composed of pulverized feldspar, carbonate of sodium (dry), calcined borax and a little oxide of tin. Thus prepared, the pots are gradually dried, and then the glaze is fired or fused under a muffle at a bright red heat.

Some oxide of lead is occasionally added to the above mixture, but though it increases the fusibility of the glaze, it impairs its value, since it will not resist the action of acids in cooking.

LUSTRE—DEAD ON GOLD AND SILVER.

To give a dead lustre to articles of gold and silver use a scratch-brush made of finely-spun glass threads.

LUSTRE FOR TIN.

If any article of tin be subjected to rapid scouring with the use of potash lye and some hard substance, a very satisfactory lustre can be obtained.

LUSTRELESS SURFACES ON STEEL.

To give a finely polished lustreless surface on tempered steel, rub the article along a smooth iron surface with pulverized oil stone until it is perfectly even and smooth. Next lay it on a sheet of white paper and rub forward and backward until a fine dead polish is acquired. Depressions or screw-holes in the steel are to be first polished and cleaned with a piece of wood and oil stone. The lustreless surface obtained by this method is very sensitive and is to be rinsed with pure soft water only. If a more lasting polish is desired, the steel surface should first be smoothed with an iron polisher and some powdered oil stone should be carefully washed and rinsed. Then some fresh oil and powdered oil stone should be stirred together in a small vessel, into which should be dipped the end of a piece of elder pith, and the steel surface polished with a mild pressure. The end of the pith being cut off as soon as it becomes soiled. As a final step, the article should be thoroughly cleaned with soft water, which will give it a fine, white, lustreless polish.

LUSTROUS BLACK FOR BRASS.

A lustrous black on brass is secured by the dissolution of carbonate of copper, which has been freshly precipitated while yet moist in strong liquid ammonia, enough of copper salt being used so that there will be a small undissolved residue. This carbonate of copper is made by mixing when hot a solution of equal portions of soda and cupric sulphate, then filtering same and washing off the precipitation. This solution of copper salt in ammonia is to be diluted with ¼ its volume of water, to which the addition is made of 31 to 46 grains of graphite and the mass heated to 95 degrees or 104 degrees Fahrenheit. Clean the brass and put it in this pickle for a brief time (a minute or so) until it shows a full black shade, then rinse same in water, followed by an immersion in hot water, and dry it in sawdust. As the solution does not keep, no more should be made at a time than is necessary for immediate use.

MAKING HOLES IN HARD STEEL.

To make a hole in hard steel use a compound consisting of ½ teaspoonful powdered salt, 1 gill vinegar, 20 drops nitric acid, 1 ounce sulphate of copper and ¼ ounce alum.

MAKING JOINTS SOUND.

For making metallic joints sound, use a putty made of boiled linseed oil and red lead. Or, use a putty of equal parts of white and red lead.

MAKING PLATINUM ADHERE TO GOLD.

If you desire to make platinum adhere to gold, a small quantity of 18-karat gold should be sweated into the surface of the platinum at almost a white heat in order that the gold may soak into the face of the platinum. The face thus secured is one to which ordinary solder will firmly adhere.

MALLEABLE BRASS.

Thirty-three parts of copper and 25 of zinc are alloyed, the copper being first put into the crucible, which is loosely covered. As soon as the copper is melted, zinc, purified by sulphur, is added. The alloy is then cast into molding sand in the shape of bars.

MALLEABLE BRITANNIA METAL.

Malleable Britannia Metal is composed of

1 part Bismuth,
48 parts Zinc,
3 parts Copper,
48 parts Tin.

MANUFACTURE OF KNIVES FROM OLD FILES.

To make knives from old files, first draw the temper from the file by heating it to a cherry red. Then put in ashes of about 5 inches on the forge, leaving it there until it becomes cool. Next grind out the file-marks and then draw with a heat no higher than a bright cherry red and a smooth-faced hammer. Next draw the file slightly thicker than you desire the back of the blade to be, and bend the blade with the edge on the inside, then draw the blade to an edge. The drawing of the blade on the inner curve will straighten it. After it has been drawn to an even color and straightened, drill three holes for fastening on the handle and shape with the file. Do not make the edge too thin, or you will find tempering difficult. Use soft, warmish water for tempering. Take out the handle ends with tongs or tweezers, hold the blade with the back down over a clear-well-charred fire, and heat evenly to the first hole until the blade becomes red, then immerse same endwise in water. After this is done the blade should be in such condition that when tried with a file the latter will take hold just a little. If this test shows the blade to be too hard, dip same in linseed oil and hold over a clear, slow fire until the ignition of the oil, when it is to be dipped into water again. This will bring about toughening and cause it to hold its edge better.

MANUFAOTURE OF METAL PIPES.

To make metal pipes, bend a piece of soft steel to a pipe so that both edges lie close together, then polish same and coat with copper in a suitable cyanide solution. If a layer of copper of special thickness is desired it should be treated in a solution of cupric sulphate. Then coat the pipe with brass in a cyanide solution and then polish. This system will give a metallic-coated pipe, without any soldering or welding.

MARBLING ZINC.

To secure the effect of marble on zinc, moisten the gray zinc and apply hydro-chloric acid in spots with a sponge, then rinse off, and while still wet pour over it an acidified solution of sulphate of copper, which will produce the appearance of black marble. This having a dull surface should undergo a coat of varnish.

MATCHES—FRICTION.

To make matches, take 8 parts (by weight) gum arabic, 5 parts phosphorus, 7 parts nitre, 8 parts powdered peroxide of manganese. Make a mucilage of the gum and water, then add the manganese, then the phosphorus, and heat them to about 130 degrees Fahrenheit. When the phosphorus is melted add the nitre, and stir the whole thoroughly until the mass becomes a uniform paste. The matches, the ends of which have been previously dipped in sulphur, are then dipped in the composition and dried in the air. Friction papers for the pocket or matches for parlor and bedroom use may be made by adding some gum benzoin to the mucilage, which will give an agreeable odor when the matches are ignited.

MELTING GUTTA PERCHA.

Gutta percha is readily dissolved in boiling spirits of turpentine, or in coal tar or naphtha. Practically, it cannot be melted. For all mechanical purposes it is shaved to a thin consistency, then thrown into a steam-heated tank or vessel, where it is rendered soft. The mass is then transferred into a sort of mangling machine, which tears it into shreds, then it is softened to a dough-like consistency by being immersed in hot water, after which it is kneaded in heated hollow cylinders which revolve and mix the plastic mass and give to it a uniform pasty consistency. It is then passed through heated rollers, coming out much like rolled pie-crust, when it can be worked into any desired form, and is afterwards hardened by being slowly dried before a proper heat.

MENDING FILES.

To mend a file have a little bottle of muriate of zinc and wet the break with it immediately; then heat a soldering iron and tin the ends of the file. Heat the file pretty warm—not enough to start the temper, but rather too hot to hold in the hand. When well tinned and hot, press the two pieces firmly together, squeeze out nearly all the solder, and let the file cool. Trim off the joint. Let it lay a day or two, or, in damp weather, even an hour or two, and you can never mend it so it will stay. Take it the minute it snaps and you can mend it.

MENDING GRANITE WARE.

To mend granite ironware, place the article to be mended upon a piece of iron, so that it will be perfectly solid, and pound the rivet down flat, being careful to strike only the rivet, as a blow on the granite ware would cause the enamel to cleave off.

(2) Place the article to be repaired on something firm and with a chisel or other tool peck off about one-quarter of an inch around the hole. Scrape with a knife or scraper until bright. Flux with moder-

ately strong acid and solder all the bright space the granite has been broken from.

MENDING IRON POTS AND PANS.

To mend iron pots and pans, partially melt two parts of sulphur and add one part of fine black lead. Mix well, pour on stone, cool and break in pieces. Use like solder with an iron.

(2) Mix finest sifted lime with some white of an egg till a thin kind of paste is formed; then add some iron filings. Apply this to the fracture and the vessel will be found nearly as sound as ever.

MENDING STOVE LINING.

A good method for mending stove lining is the following: Take powdered soapstone and salt in equal parts, wet with water, which will make an everlasting and fireproof mending for the lining of stoves. It is very much less expensive and troublesome to procure and put in place than new firebricks. Don't let fire spoil the stove because the brick needs mending.

MERCURIC NITRATE.

Mercuric nitrate is made by the dissolution, at a gentle heat, of mercury and nitric acid.

MERCURY—TEST FOR.

To test mercury, put a drop in a dish and pour nitric acid over the same. If the mercury be pure it will give a slight movement for a minute, and thereafter remain quiet and without motion. If it contains foreign metals a vigorous circular motion will be at once commenced and kept up until the dissolution of the mercury is completed.

METAL FLUID FOR PLASTER PARIS MOLD IMPRESSIONS.

The following is a metal that becomes a fluid readily and is suitable for making impressions of plaster of Paris molds, wood engravings, etc.: Tin (3 parts), lead (13 parts), bismuth (6 parts). Tin (2 parts), lead

(3 parts), bismuth (5 parts). Tin (1 part), lead (1 part), bismuth (2 parts). Tin (3 parts), lead (5 parts), bismuth (8 parts).

METALLINE.

Metalline is an alloy composed of 35 parts cobalt, 25 parts aluminum, 10 parts iron and 30 parts copper.

METALS—FUSIBLE.

(1) Take bismuth, 8 lbs.; lead, 5 lbs.; tin, 3 lbs. Melt together. This alloy fuses below 212 degrees.

(2) Take bismuth, 2 lbs.; lead, 5 lbs.; tin, 3 lbs. Melt. This alloy fuses in boiling water.

(3) Take lead, 3 lbs.; tin, 2 lbs.; bismuth, 5 lbs. Fusible at 197 degrees.

In each of the three foregoing receipts melt the tin and lead first, then remove from the fire and add the bismuth.

METHOD OF COPPERING TIN.

The ingredients given below are those required to make one gallon of the solution:

Take first 1 gallon of clean water, which bring to the boiling point, then dissolve in it 8 ounces of sulphate of copper crystals; after this is thoroughly dissolved, add 2 fluid ounces of aqua ammonia; to this add 8 ounces of cyanide of potassium. This solution should be allowed to stand over night. Rolled sheet copper should be hung in the solution, and the metal to be plated should hang in the middle of the vat, near the rolled sheet copper. This solution can be used either with electric batteries or electric dynamos. Before the metal is hung in the vat it should be cleaned off thoroughly in a potash solution. This solution is made by mixing 2 1-pound cans of lye in 20 gallons of clean, warm water. When the metal is thoroughly cleaned in this warm potash it should then be rinsed in clean water; then it is to be hung in the vat, the current turned on and plated. If hung too long in the vat the copper will blister and peel off. When the article plated is removed from the vat it should be immersed in boiling hot water, then dried and afterwards buffed, if a polish is wanted.

MINARGENT.

Minargent is an alloy consisting of

5 parts Antimony,
2 parts Aluminum,
70 parts Nickel,
100 parts Copper.

MINERAL GREEN.

A mineral green is made by the addition of a solution of soda to one of cupric sulphate. It is poisonous.

MINOFOR METAL.

Minofor metal is an alloy consisting of

66 parts Tin,
20 parts Antimony,
9 parts Zinc,
4 parts Copper,
1 part Iron.

or

67 53-100 parts Tin,
17 parts Antimony,
8 94-100 parts Zinc,
3 26-100 parts Copper.

MOIRE METALLIQUE.

In order to give tinplate a crystalline surface, polishing it by hammering and then heat over a coal fire, so that the tin will melt without oxidation, then remove same, and water is poured over the side which has been exposed to the fire, from a vessel so arranged that a broad stream can be focused on the surface. As it cools the tin crystallizes, but a poor appearance is presented by the surface and it is necessary, therefore, to give it further treatment with acid. Place the sheet in a compound of 2 parts hydrochloric acid, 1 part nitric acid, and 3 parts water. This will cause the dissolution of the tin upon the surface in a little while, then take the sheet out, wash it in caustic potash lye in order to enhance the metallic lustre, and rinse in water, dry at a moderate heat and then coat with transparent copal lacquer. If it is desired, the direction of crystallization may be determined by the surface manipulations; for instance, draw designs on the back of the heated and cooled plate, with a hot soldering iron and the tin will melt through the plate and the reaction of the design on the side can be made, owing to the action of the acid changing the direction of the crystallization. If tinned sheet-iron is heated over the flame of a spirit lamp the tin will fuse all around and a round spot will be formed, whose circumference will vary according to the time the sheet is held over the flame. When the flame is removed the place of its application will be recognized as a center of stellated crystallization. Pure tin is best for this purpose. The moire is, as a rule, obtained by the exposure of tin which is carefully cleaned, to the action of sulphuric acid, nitric acid or hydro-chloric acid, the surface covered with moire being finally freed, as much as possible, from the oxides produced during the continuance of the operation.

MOSAIC GOLD.

Mosaic gold is a copper-zinc alloy composed of

65 3-10 parts Copper,
34 7-10 parts Zinc.

MUCILAGE.

To prepare mucilage, such as is sold in stationery stores: Dextrine, 2 parts; acetic acid, 1 part; water, 5 parts; alcohol, 1 part.

MUCILAGE FOR LABELING TIN.

A good mucilage for sticking labels on tin is one of the popular wants of the day. Every little while, also, formulas or methods are published, and we should judge from this that many of the methods given are not very satisfactory. We give below some of the most general methods suggested.

The addition of about 3 or 4 per cent. aluminum sulphate (not alum), or, better still, about 10 per cent. of butter of antimony, is said to greatly improve the adhesiveness of the mucilage. Others have suggested roughening the surface with acids in small degree on applying to the tin; thus, honey, flour, treacle, etc., have come into use as seen in formula No. 1.

(1) Make gum tragacanth into a mucilage of the desired consistency with hot water, and then add to it 10 per cent. of flour.

(2) Boil 2 pounds of flour with 1 quart of water to make a stiff paste; add 2 ounces of tartaric acid and 1 pint of molasses. Boil together until stiff and add 10 drops of carbolic acid.

(3) Shellac, 2 parts; borax, 1 part; water, 16 parts, are boiled together until the shellac dissolves.

(4) Add 1 ounce of dammar varnish to 4 ounces of tragacanth paste.

(5) Roughen the surface with emery paper, then apply the label, preferably with water glass as an adhesive agent.

(6) Balsam of fir, 1 part; turpentine, 3 parts. Dissolve. This is only applicable with good qualities of well-sized labels.

(7) Clean the surface by rubbing with a solution of caustic potash and then thoroughly wipe before applying the label. This is employed on the principle of attributing the difficulty to the presence of a thin film of grease, and is also the case with the addition of water of ammonia to the paste.

(8) Brush the surface over with a thin streak of butter of antimony, or with oleate of mercury, clean well, and apply the label.

(9) Brush over with strong tannin solution, allow to dry and apply the label, previously well gummed.

(10) Apply Venice turpentine to good starch paste.

(11) Soften good glue with water and then dissolve in it acetic acid of 10 per cent. strength.

(12) About 15 per cent. of glycerine added to the paste is said to work admirably.

MUNTZ METAL.

Muntz metal is a copper-zinc alloy composed of

60 parts Copper,
40 parts Zinc.

NEOGEN.

Neogen is an alloy consisting of

½ part Aluminum,
½ part Bismuth,
2 parts Tin,
12 parts Nickel,
27 parts Zinc,
58 parts Copper.

NEWTON'S METAL

Is composed of tin (3 parts), lead (5 parts), bismuth (8 parts).

NICKEL-ALUMINUM.

Nickel-aluminum is an alloy composed of 20 parts nickel and 8 parts aluminum, used for decorative threads.

NICKEL CHLORINE.

Nickel chlorine is obtained by the dissolution in aqua regia of metallic nickel.

NICKEL HARD LEAD.

Nickel hard lead is an alloy composed of 100 parts type metal and 5 parts nickel, used for types.

NICKELING.

To nickel, use a bath of 2 pounds of the double sulphate of nickel and ammonium and 1 pound of refined boracic acid. Boil fifteen minutes and then cool.

NICKELING ZINC.

To nickel zinc amalgamate the zinc first in a solution of chloride or nitrate of mercury, acidulated with sulphuric or muriatic acid. By this means a feeble current of electricity will answer the purpose.

NICKEL NITRIC.

Nickel nitric is a deliquescent emerald-green powder obtained by the dissolution of nickel in nitric acid.

NICKEL PLATING ON ZINC.

In nickel plating zinc the zinc is cleansed by dilute hydrochloric acid and thoroughly washed. It is then hung in the nickel bath for a short time, and on taking out is rinsed and thoroughly scraped, so removing all that does not adhere firmly. This is repeated until the zinc is covered with a thin film of nickel, which can afterward be made as thick as required. The suitable current strength is easily found. When the zinc is once thoroughly covered, the current may be increased without any risk of peeling off.

NICKEL SULPHATE.

Nickel sulphate is obtained by the dissolution of nickel in sulphuric acid. The action of the acid is hastened if a few drops of nitric acid are added thereto.

NITRATE OF SILVER.

Nitrate of silver is made by the dissolution of silver in moderately diluted nitric acid and the concentration of the solution after it has separated out in anhydrous table.

NON-RUSTING COATING.

A coating which does not oxidize readily upon steel and iron wire is made by the immersion of the wire in weak acid solution, then washing same and drying it at 176 degrees Fahrenheit. The wire is then to be plunged in a fluid alloy consisting of

9 parts Lead,
1 part Silver,
90 parts Tin.

NURNBERG GOLD.

Nurnberg gold is an alloy consisting of

90 per cent. Copper,
7½ per cent. Aluminum,
2½ per cent. Gold.

ORANGE LUMINOUS PAINTS.

For orange luminous paints, 46 parts varnish are mixed with 17.6 parts prepared barium sulphate, 1 part powdered Indian yellow, 1.5 parts prepared madder lake, and 38 parts luminous calcium sulphide.

OROIDE.

Oroide is a copper-zinc alloy composed of

90 parts Copper,
10 parts Zinc,
or
85 5-10 parts Copper,
14 5-10 parts Zinc.

OXIDIZING SILVER OR COPPER.

To make a liquid that will oxidize silver a glossy black by dipping small articles in the liquid: Use a solution of sulphide of potassium; polish metal before. and rub with a soft rag or chamois after immersion. To make a liquid that will oxidize copper or oroide by dipping to imitate bronze: Use the same bath. but have it quite dilute. If for outside work, simply oil with olive oil, and let the weather do the rest.

OXIDIZING ZINC.

The color of zinc may be changed by immersing the zinc in a mixture of 100 parts sulphuric acid, 100 parts nitric acid, and common salt 1 per cent. After remaining a little while in the mixture it acquires a dead lustre; this will become a bright one if the object is plunged in several times, and rinsed as often, in the same compound.

PAINT FOR TIN POTS.

For a good paint for tin pots use the following: Make a thick varnish of shellac dissolved in naphtha or methylated spirit. Two or three coats should be applied.

PAINT FOR TIN ROOFING.

A good paint for a tin roof is made from common Spanish brown, Venetian red, or yellow ochre, mixed with either pure raw linseed oil, or equal parts linseed and fish oil; the only partial drying of the latter causing a degree of elasticity in the coat of paint which prevents its cracking during the expansion and contraction of the metal.

PAINT FOR TIN ROOF AND FOR IRON.

The best paint for tin roof—a paint which will preserve the tin and stand wear, also is a good paint for iron: Pure linseed oil, or, as some prefer, equal parts of linseed oil and good fish oil, should form the body, with which may be incorporated Spanish brown, Venetian red and yellow ochre. This should be laid on in good body. Only the best materials should be used to paint iron surfaces. Pure linseed oil without the admixture of any volatile oil should be used for the body. The large percentage of linolein which it contains combines with the oxygen of the air and forms a solid translucent substance which possesses much substance and elasticity, and will not crack or blister, by reason of the expansion and contraction of the iron with the variations of the temperature. It is very adhesive and impervious to water. Red lead with linseed oil makes a specially good paint, though other colors may be used. Asphalt or pitch dissolved in turpentine or petroleum and mixed with a portion of linseed oil also make a durable paint for iron.

PAINTING ZINC.

To make paint adhere to sheet zinc: Made a mordant as follows: One part chloride of copper, 1 of nitrate of copper, and 1 of sal-ammoniac, dissolved in

64 parts of water, to which add one part of commercial hydrochloric acid. The sheets of zinc should be brushed over with this liquid, when they will assume a dark color. After they are dry they can be painted, and the paint will not be affected by changes of the weather.

PAINT—LUMINOUS.

This useful paint may, it is said, be made by the following simple method: Take oyster shells and clean them with warm water; put them into the fire for half an hour; at the end of that time take them out and let them cool. When quite cool, pound them fine, and take away any gray parts, as they are of no use. Put the powder in a crucible in alternate layers with flour and sulphur. Put on the lid and cement with sand made into a stiff paste with beer. When dry, put over the fire and bake for an hour. Wait until quite cold before opening the lid. The product ought to be white. You must separate all gray parts, as they are not luminous. Make a sifter in the following manner: Take a pot, put a piece of very fine muslin very loosely across it, tie around with a string, put the powder into the top, and rake about until only the coarse powder remains; open the pot and you will find a very small powder; mix it into a thin paint with gum water, as two thin applications are better than one thick one. This will give a paint that will remain luminous far into the night, provided it is exposed to light during the day.

PAINTS—LUMINOUS OIL-COLOR.

For making gray oil-color luminous paint and a yellowish-brown oil-color luminous paint, take pure linseed oil, cold-press it and thicken by heat.

Then for the gray paint: Take 45 parts of oil, mix with 6 parts prepared barium sulphate, 6 parts prepared calcium carbonate, .05 part ultramarine blue, 6.5 parts gray zinc sulphide.

For the yellowish-brown oil-color luminous paint, take 48 parts of the pure linseed oil, 10 parts precipitated barium sulphate, 8 parts auripigment, and 34 parts luminous calcium sulphide.

PAPER—FIREPROOF.

Fireproof paper may be made from a pulp consisting of 1 part of vegetable fibre, 2 parts of asbestos, 1-10 part borax, 1-5 part of alum. The ink is made from 85 parts of graphite, .8 part of copal varnish, 7.5 parts of copperas, 30 parts of tincture of nutgalls, and a sufficient quantity of indigo carmine.

PASTE FOR CLEANING BRASS.

Rotten stone, 4½ pounds; oxalic acid (dissolved in water), 2 ounces; soft soap, 8 ounces; sweet oil, 8 ounces; boiling water, 1 pound; spirits of turpentine, 1 ounce. Mix.

PASTE FOR FURNACE PIPES.

Well-prepared bill-stickers' paste is as good as anything we know of for pasting asbestos to tin hot air or furnace pipes, and will not scale off when the pipes are heated.

PASTE FOR LABELS.

Here is a receipt for fastening labels on tin which makes a strong mucilage: Soften good glue (fish glue is most tenacious) in water; then boil it with strong vinegar and thicken the liquid, during boiling, with fine wheat flour, so that a paste results; or starch paste, with which a little Venice turpentine has been incorporated while it was warm.

PASTE METAL POLISH.

A "paste" metal polish for cleaning and polishing brass is thus made: Oxalic acid, 1 part; iron peroxide, 15 parts; powdered rotten stone, 20 parts; palm oil, 60 parts; petroleum, 4 parts. See that solids are thoroughly pulverized and sifted, then add and thoroughly incorporate oil and petrolatum.

PASTING LABELS ON TIN.

For pasting labels on tin, use the following:

(1) Four parts shellac, 2 parts borax, 30 parts water; boil until the shellac is dissolved.

(2) Add 4 ounces dammar varnish to 1 pound of tragacanth mucilage.

(3) Balsam of fir, 1 part; turpentine, 3 parts; use only for varnished labels.

(4) Butter of antimony is good to prepare the tin for the label.

(5) Venice turpentine added to good starch paste makes an excellent mounting medium.

(6) A paste for pasting paper on tin is composed of the following: Dissolve rye flour in a solution of caustic soda, dilute with water, and in so doing stir all the time. To this paste add Venetian turpentine—a few drops to each half pound of flour.

PASTE—STOVE.

To make a good stove paste: Dissolve ordinary laundry soap to about the consistency of soft soap and add sufficient plumbago and carbon black to make it just thick enough to pour while hot.

PASTE STOVE POLISH.

Put enough plumbago into black varnish to thicken it. Thin with benzine or gasolene, and polish before dry.

(2) A good paste polish is made by using 2 pounds plumbago, 5 gills Japan dryer or furniture varnish, 1 gill asphaltum varnish, and thin down for use with gasolene; or, can omit the asphalt and use lampblack, a trial of which will determine the quantity. Mix as you want to use the polish.

(3) For cracks in stoves, finely pulverized iron (procured at a drug store) made into a thick paste with water-glass. The hotter the fire the more the cement melts and combines, and the more completely does the crack become closed.

PEWTER BRITANNIA METAL.

Pewter Britannia metal is composed of

1 15-100 parts Lead,
1 6-10 parts Copper,
5 7-100 parts Antimony,
81 2-10 parts Tin,

or

1 8-10 parts Lead,
1 8-10 parts Copper,
7 6-10 parts Antimony,
89 3-10 parts Tin,

or

1 6-10 parts Bismuth,
3 6-100 parts Zinc,
1 6-10 parts Copper,
6 6-10 parts Antinomy,
83 3-10 parts Tin.

PHOSPHIDE OF COPPER.

Phosphide of copper is made by heating together a mixture of 2 parts of granulated copper, 1 part of finely pulverized coal, and 4 parts of super-phosphate of lime in a crucible, the temperature being moderate. The melted phosphide of copper containing 14 per cent. of phosphorus will separate on the bottom of the crucible. Another method is to prepare phosphide of copper by the addition of phosphorus, by a copper sulphide solution, and boiling same, and sulphur to be added as the sulphide is precipitated. The precipitation is carefully dried, melted and cast into ingots. These ingots, when in perfect condition, are very black.

PHOSPHIDE OF TIN.

To prepare phosphide of tin, place a bar of zinc in an aqueous solution of chloride of tin. The sponge-like tin particles, that are separated, are poured when moist into a crucible, upon whose bottom sticks of phosphorus have been placed. The tin is then pressed tightly into the crucible and submitted to moderate warmth. This heating is to continue until the flames of burning phosphorus die out. After the operation is done there is found on the bottom of the crucible a coarse, crystalline mass, of a white color, consisting of a pure phosphide of tin.

PICKLING BRASS.

To pickle brass, heat the article in a muffle at a dark-red heat and then dip same in diluted sulphuric acid, in order to produce a clean metallic surface. After this heating and immersion, throw the article to be pickled in a tub filled with weak and impure nitric acid. This tub, or trough, is generally constructed of wood lined with lead plates, and is filled with nitric acid that may, perhaps, be best designated as second ground, as it has been used before for stronger baths. The articles when pure and of uniform color should be taken from the bath and rinsed in water, then dried in sawdust. They are next deadened. The way this is accomplished is by putting them into a nitric acid bath, diluted with about one-third water. The dipped articles acquire a coat that looks like a milky scum, which vanishes after a minute or two. Absolute uniformity is vital, and when this is obtained the articles should be immersed in strong nitric acid, this being followed up by dipping them in a number of baths of water, in order to take away all traces of acid. If the articles contain depressions which might retain acid, it must be rapidly dipped in a warm potash solution. The article when washed should be allowed to lie in clean water, to which an addition of crude pulverized tartar has been made. This method of treatment gives them the beautiful dead color on which so high a valuation is commonly placed. If it is desired to pickle the articles so they will show lustre, they should be placed at once, after being cleaned, in strong nitric acid; and should the very highest degree of lustre be desired, the entire surface should be thoroughly gone over with a scratch-brush. To polish same finely polished steel tools should be used, the articles then to be brushed over with ox-gall, and during the process be occasionally dipped in water to which a little tartar has been added. Then dry same in wood shavings in an iron pan over a heated hearth, lacquered with cold shellac solution, which can be colored by alkanet, dragon's blood, etc.

PICKLING CASTINGS.

For pickling casting to remove the scale prepare a bath in a vessel (lined with lead) of 3 parts muriatic acid to 1 of water, and leave from five to twenty minutes.

PICKLING GERMAN SILVER.

To pickle particles of German silver, first dip them in a compound of 12 parts of water and 1 part of nitric acid. The next step is to quickly immerse them in a compound of equal parts of sulphuric acid and nitric acid, and then rinse them in water, finally drying them in pine sawdust. This is a delicate operation, and very great care should be taken to see that the acid is not too strong or that the articles do not stay in the bath too long, as in either case great loss and damage would ensue by the dissolution of the metal. To stop the articles from rusting, wash them repeatedly with clean water and dry carefully.

PICKLING ZINC.

To pickle zinc, scour it with sand and powdered pumice and apply a solution of potassium-ammonium tartrate thickened with sufficient clay to form a fluid paste. After allowing a few hours to elapse rub the articles with a brush dipped from time to tine into fine sand wet with the pickle.

PINCHBECK.

Pinchbeck is a copper-zinc alloy composed of

93 6-10 parts Copper,
6 4-10 parts Zinc.

PLATING WITH PLATINUM.

To plate with platinum, the clean metallic surface is

planished and rubbed with a solution of 1 part platinum chloride, dissolved in 15 parts alcohol, and 50 parts ether, and when dry polished in a warm place with a dry cotton or woolen cloth. Bad places in platinum plating may be made good in a similar manner. The coating resembles steel in appearance, and imparts to bronze, brass or copper utensils a fine platinum surface.

PLATINIDE.

Platinide is an alloy composed of 60 parts platinum, 35 parts nickel, 2 parts gold, and 3 parts iron, used for crucibles and chemical utensils.

PLUMBER'S SOIL.

To make plumber's soil, boil glue slowly in water until it is all dissolved. This, of course, will give you a thin solution of glue. Then stir in enough lampblack to make the mass the consistency of paste, simmering the paste over a slow fire for the space of half an hour. Pursue the following method in testing your compound: Apply it with a brush to a piece of lead and allow it to get cool; then bend the lead backward and forward in the hand in order to judge of its adhesiveness. If it cracks while the lead is undergoing the process, there is too much glue in the compound, and it is n. g. If, on the other hand, it does not crack and adheres to the lead, it is all right.

POLISH FOR PRESSED ARTICLES OF BRASS.

For polish for pressed articles of brass, use an agent consisting of equal volumes of ox-gall and water boiled together. Keep the fluid, when cold, in a well-corked bottle, and, when using same, pour it into a glass or porcelain vessel.

POLISHING ANTIMONY.

Polish antimony with burnt magnesia upon soft leather or with fine jewelers' rouge.

POLISHING ARTICLES OF STEEL, GILT, BRONZE, GOLD, ETC.

Jewelers' rouge is artificially made as follows: Pulverized saltpetre and common salt are mixed with pulverized green vitriol, the compound being stirred with water to a paste and boiled down to dryness in a crucible. This compound is heated in a Hessian crucible to a red heat until it becomes homogeneous and quiet. Then it is poured out, and, when cool, powdered, boiled with water, and washed. This powder should be slightly elutriated for the elimination of grains of sand which may have been imparted to it from the crucible. Collect the powder on a cloth and dry same. As a substitution for 50 parts of crystallized green vitriol, 25 parts of pure nitrate of soda, 18 parts of sodium sulphate and 13 parts of common salt may be employed. If more saltpetre is used the preparation has a reddish tinge, while an addition of the amount of potash sulphate gives it a more violet color. An addition of salt makes it browner and the jewelers' rouge is obtained in the lustrous lamina. A second method consists in the dissolution, in 4 parts of water, of 1 part of soda and the heating of this solution to the boiling point, gradually stirring into the boiling fluid a little more than ½ part of green vitriol, and continue the boiling. After the substance is cold, on the bottom of the vessel will be found a greenish-white mass of ferrous carbonate. The super-natant fluid is then poured off, the precipitation is washed in an abundance of water and then dried and converted into red ferric oxide by a little glowing in a crucible.

POLISHING BALLS FOR SILVER.

Polishing balls for silver are given their form by means of an agglutinant. It is made by thoroughly stirring together 5 parts of whiting and 2 parts of yellow tripoli and working the mixture together with a solution of 1 part gum-arabic in 12 parts of water, until it becomes a stiff paste, and this is formed into balls (with the hands) about as big as the egg of an ordinary pigeon. These balls should be dried in moderately warm room, and after their perfect calidification should be packed in tin foil.

POLISHING BRASS.

To polish brass, use ordinary whiting or chalk and a damp cotton or woolen cloth. If the metal is stained or tarnished, then use rotten stone and oil on a cloth, and finish with whiting for a gloss. If corroded and blackened, use oxalic acid in water with the rotten stone, instead of oil.

POLISHING BRASS, COPPER AND TOMBAC.

First plunge the articles in nitric acid and then wash rapidly in a large quantity of water, then dip them with constant movement for a few seconds in a mixture which has been allowed to stand at least twelve hours, composed of

53	ounces	Sulphuric Acid,
70½	ounces	Nitric Acid,
2 82-100	ounces	Hydro-chloric Acid,
3 17-100	ounces	Sal-ammoniac,
5 29-100	ounces	Alum,
3½	ounces	Lampblack.

Take the articles from this bath and wash same rapidly in a large quantity of water. The method of preparing this bath is as follows: First pour the nitric acid into the vessel, next adding the finely pulverized salts, followed by the hydro-chloric acid, and after an hour or so, gradually add the sulphuric acid. Care should be taken in mixing these acids, as a large amount of heat is originated and fumes injurious to the lungs are developed; hence, the mixture is best made out of doors or under a chimney with an excellent draught. A large vessel should be used, because otherwise the sulphuric acid might run over. This mixture can be used for a considerably long time, as it is only necessary to add a little sulphuric acid and by and by a little nitric acid and sal-ammoniac.

(2) Brass, copper, tombac and gold and silver are polished with Vienna lime and oil.

POLISHING CARTRIDGES.

To polish cartridges, wet 10 parts of emery dust and 50 parts of elutriated quartz with 100 parts of a 30 per cent. gum tragacanth solution, the mass being given the requisite consistency with a solution of 100 parts of soap dissolved in 150 parts spirits of wine.

(2) Infusorial earth, either alone or impregnated with oleic, is a good polish for cartridges.

POLISHING COPPER.

Copper parts are polished by rubbing them with rotten stone and oil, followed by an application of a flannel rag, and finally with leather. If a solution of oxalic acid is applied to dull brass, the layer of oxide is quickly removed and the metal uncovered. The next step is to wash off the acid with water and rub the brass with soft leather.

Articles plunged in a solution of hydro-chloric acid with alum, triturated with water for a few seconds, are given a golden color. A pretty color, ranging between orange and gold, is given polished copper by its brief immersion in a solution of crystallized acetate of copper. A violet color is given copper by its brief plunging in a solution of chloride of antimony, followed by its rubbing with a stick enwrapped with cotton.

POLISHING GOLD.

Polish gold with jewelers' rouge, mixed with alcohol, and applied to the buff-stick.

POLISHING IRON AND STEEL.

Before polishing iron and steel, treat them with emery, then use either tin, putty, Vienna lime or oxide of iron, either the polishing material or the article being wet with water or a spirit.

POLISHING METALS.

The first step in the polishing of metals consists in rubbing down the surface by some hard material that will produce a series of scratches in all directions, the level of which is practically identical, and which obliterate file-marks. For this purpose pumice and water or sand and water applied upon a piece of soft wood is used. After the removal of the first coarse marks the next step is the removal of the marks left by the first polishing material by means of finely-powdered pumice-stone ground up with olive oil. To proceed with the polishing even finer powders are next used, such as tripoli and rotten stone. For the higher degree of polish putty of tin and crocus martis are also used. The entire process consists simply in the removal of the coarse scratches by the substitution of those which are finer and finer, until you can no longer see them with the naked eye. And even quite a while after, should the surface be subjected to a microscopic examination, it can be seen that the surface which did not appear to have any scratches is covered all over with an infinite number of them, all of which are so infinitesimal as to require a high magnifier for their discovery. A great care is absolutely essential to have the last polishing material uniformly fine, for if, by any mischance, a single grain of any coarse substance is mixed with it, visible scratches instead of a perfectly polished surface will be produced.

POLISHING NICKEL WATCH MOVEMENTS.

To polish nickel watch movements which have become stained, add 1 part of sulphuric acid to 50 parts of rectified alcohol, and place the parts to be polished in this fluid for about 15 seconds, immersing also only a few at a time so as to be enabled to take them out at the proper time, a longer immersion being harmful. After taking them from this bath, rinse the parts in clean water and put them for a few minutes in rectified alcohol; then dry them in sawdust or with soft linen. Nickel watch movements which have been cleaned by this method have practically the appearance of being new, as their smooth surface is not marred at all, as would be the case if a file were used.

POLISHING PASTE.

A scouring paste, said to be of the very best, consists of oxalic acid, 1 part; iron peroxide, 15 parts; powdered rotten stone, 20 parts; palm oil, 60 parts; petrolatum, 4 parts. Pulverize the oxalic acid and add rouge and rotten stone, mixing thoroughly, and sift to remove all grit; then add gradually the palm oil and petrolatum, incorporating thoroughly. Add oil of myrbane or oil of lavender to suit.

POLISHING PASTE FOR BRASS.

A good polishing paste for brass is made by the dissolution, in 120 parts of boiling water, of 15 parts oxalic acid, and to this is added 500 parts of pumice powder, 60 parts salt soap, 60 parts of any kind of fat and 7 parts of oil of turpentine.

POLISHING PASTE FOR SILVERING.

For a polish paste for silver, take a few drops of essence of mirbane and perfume with same 3 parts of vaseline, mixing into this 1 part of burnt hartshorn, 1 part cuttle-bone (pulverized), and 5 parts whiting, so that a thorough compound of the consistency of butter is obtained.

POLISHING POMADE.

A polishing pomade is mixed by stirring 5 pounds fine colcothar into a heated mixture of 1 pound of lard and 4 pounds American mineral oil.

(2) Mix 1 pound fine colcothar into a melted mass consisting of 5 pounds yellow vaseline.

(3) Melt 2 pounds vaseline and 2 pounds palm oil, and into this melted mass stir 14 11-100 ounces of tripoli, ¾ ounces oxalic acid, 1 pound ferric oxide. Any of these pomades can be nicely perfumed by the use of a little essence of mirbane.

POLISHING POWDER FOR GOLD.

A polishing powder for gold consists of

17 4-10 parts Chalk,
4 3-10 parts Alumina,
1 7-10 parts Carbonate of Magnesia,
4 3-10 parts Carbonate of Lead,
1 7-10 parts Jewelers' Rouge,
2 6-10 parts Silica.

Another polish for gold articles is made by the dissolution of iron filings in hydro-chloric acid, until gas ceases developing. The resultant chloride of iron should be compounded with liquid ammonia as long as a precipitation is made. This precipitation should be collected and dried without further washing, at a temperature which will prevent the adhesive ammonia from volatilization. This converts the ferrous oxide, originally precipitated, into ferric, and the resultant mixture is composed of 30 per cent. of ammonia and 70 per cent. of ferric oxide.

POLISHING POWDER—FOR GOLDSMITHS.

Take 7 parts sesquioxide of iron, 3 parts sal-ammoniac. Mix thoroughly.

POLISHING POWDER FOR SILVER.

A polishing powder for silver consists of

8 parts Flake White,
2 parts Pulverized Alum,
4 parts Cream of Tartar (finely pulverized).

Mixed and worked into a stiff paste with strong wine vinegar and then dried in ammonia. The dry mass is pulverized, worked again to a paste with vinegar. This is done once again after drying, and the resultant substance is pulverized.

A second powder is made by thoroughly mixing, by means of a sieve,

¼ part Citric Acid (pulverized),
1 part Soda,
10 parts Whiting (fine).

When it is desired to use this powder, wet it in order to effect the dissolution of the soda and citric acid, so that they may exert a chemical action upon the silver.

A third powder consists of

5 parts Chalk,
1 part Jewelers' Rouge,
1 part Pulverized Hartshorn.

POLISHING SILVER.

Polish silver with a burnisher or bloodstone, using with same either water or beer.

POLISHING SILVERED WARE.

Polish silvered and plated ware with Vienna lime.

POLISHING SILVERWARE.

To polish silverware moisten a rag or brush with a solution consisting of

40 parts Water,
2 parts Sal-ammoniac,
1 part Caustic Ammonia,
4 parts Sodium Hypo-sulphite.

POLISHING STEEL.

To polish steel, rub it with a piece of emery paper, from which some of the roughness has been removed by rubbing on an old knife.

POLISHING STEEL OBJECTS.

To polish steel objects, use a wheel or disk made of 16 parts of tin, 1 of zinc, to the flat side of which jewelers' rouge wet with alcohol is applied. Dry articles and burnish them with agate.

POLISHING SOAP.

A good polishing soap is made by stirring together 24 pounds of cocoanut oil and 12 pounds of lye at 38 to 40 degrees Be, and after the mass is polished, 3 pounds colcothar mixed with 3 pounds of water and

1 12-100 ounces spirits of sal-ammoniac is stirred into it.

(2) Mix thoroughly
5 pounds Colcothar,
1 pound Ammonium-carbonate,
with
25 pounds Liquid Cocoanut Oil Soap.

(3) Mix thoroughly
2 pounds Tripoli,
1 pound White Lead,
I pound Pulverized Alum,
1 pound Tartaric Acid,
with
25 pounds Liquid Cocoanut Oil Soap.

(4) Stir together
5 pounds Calcined Oxalite of Iron,
with
25 pounds Liquid Cocoanut Oil Soap.

(5) Pulverize with great care 332 parts of tartaric acid, 265 parts of infusorial earth and 332 parts of chalk or white bole. Free the infusorial earth and the bole or chalk from adhering pebbles by means of a sieve. Water is poured over the sifted mass in a vessel, which is then stirred thoroughly and for three or four minutes the bole, which is finely divided in the water, is poured off and the operation is repeated. After allowing the bole to settle, and decanting the supernatant water, the sediment is filtered and dried over a stove. After the preparation of the ingredients, as above, add to the mixture 200 parts of glycerine, 200 parts of water, and 25 parts of alcohol.

(6) Another polishing soap is made by compounding together 8 lbs. soda lye, of 23 degrees Be, with 25 lbs. cocoanut oil, the mixture being boiled until the formation of a clear, glue-like mass. After the soap is solid enough, 1 lb. of chalk and ½ lb. of white lead, tartar and alum, all previously converted into a fine powder, are added, the mass being poured into small molds about 10 inches long and open on top and bottom for the ready removal of a cold soap. If

desired, commercial cocoanut oil soap may be used instead of this special soap. This is the process: 5½ lbs. of coconaut oil soap are shaved finely and melted by adding water; constantly stir this melted soap and add to it 3 ounces of alum, 3 ounces of white lead, 3 ounces of tartar, 6 34-100 ounces of chalk, all of which have been finely pulverized.

POLISHING TIN.

To polish tin, use whiting or Vienna lime, the first being applied with chamois and the second with linen rags. If merely places in relief are to be polished a broad, rounded-off burnisher is applied, and as a polisher, white of egg, ox-gall diluted with water, soap water, or a decoction of soap root, is used. The articles are then washed with water slightly tinged with tartar and dried.

POLISHING WATER.

A good polishing water is secured by shaking together 1 lb. of alcohol, 8 8-100 ounces whiting, 1½ drachms spirits of sal-ammoniac.

POLISHING ZINC.

(1) To polish sheet zinc a good method is found in the following: First scrape and finally polish the zinc with pulverized wood charcoal or Vienna lime. The polished articles are generally dried in heated sawdust and after drying freed from adhering sawdust with a cotton rag or soft leather.

(2) Old zinc can hardly be made to look like new, but may be improved by scouring it with dilute acid and a scratch brush or dust of scouring brick. It may then be rubbed with some finer polishing substance.

(3) Mix 1 part of muriatic acid with 2 parts of water. Apply to the zinc and rub the same with sand until bright. Then dry well and rub with a cloth dipped in oil.

POLISH STEEL ON IRON.

Pulverize and dissolve the following articles in 1 qt. hot water: Blue vitriol, 1 oz.; borax, 1 oz.; prussiate of potash, 1 oz.; charcoal, 1 oz.; salt, ½ pt.; then add 1 gal. linseed oil, mix well, bring your iron or steel to the proper heat and cool in the solution.

It is said the manufacturer of the Judson governor paid $100 for this receipt, the object being to case-harden iron, so that it would take a bright polish like steel.

POTASSIUM FERRICYANIDE.

Potassium ferricyanide is made by allowing chlorine to act upon a solution of yellow prussiate of potash. It comes in the form of prismatic and occasionally tubular crystals.

POTIN.

Potin is a copper-zinc alloy composed of

71 9-10	parts	Copper,
24 9-10	parts	Zinc,
1 2-10	parts	Tin,
2	parts	Lead.

POWDER FOR SILVERING METALS.

A powder for silvering metal is made as follows: Nitrate of silver, 10 parts; common salt, 10 parts; cream of tartar, 30 parts; moisten with water and apply.

PRESERVATIVE FOR IRON AND STEEL.

To make a permanent preservative for iron or steel, it is best to use nothing but linseed oil, thickened with a pigment related to the metal itself, and native oxide or a roasted oxide of iron is the best for the purpose. Boiled linseed oil will form a skin, through which no oxidation can take place.

PRESERVING POLISHED IRON SURFACES.

To preserve polished iron surfaces from rust, melt together 7 parts fat (tallow), and 1 part resin, stirring the same until it cools. Apply in a half liquid state; if too stiff, thin with benzine or petroleum. It preserves the polish, and can easily be removed.

PREVENTING RUST IN IRON AND STEEL GOODS.

For the purpose of preventing steel goods and ground hollow ware, also halter chains, etc., from rusting while exhibited as samples, and which is cheap and will come off easily, caoutchouc oil is recommended. Spread it over the articles with a piece of flannel, in a very thin layer, and then allow it to dry. This will prevent the condensation of moisture. which causes rust, and can be removed by repeating the treatment and washing the articles after twelve or twenty-four hours.

PREVENTING RUST IN RUSSIA IRON.

To prevent Russia iron from rusting, take beeswax and chip very fine and dissolve in benzine; let it stand twenty-four hours before using. Apply same to iron with a very soft brush or woolen cloth.

(2) To prevent Russia iron from rusting, use the following: Add 1¾ pints of cold water to 7 ounces of quick lime. Let the mixture stand until the supernatant fluid is entirely clear; then pour this off and mix it with enough olive oil to form a thick cream, or, rather, to the consistency of melted and recongealed butter. Grease your articles with this and then wrap them up in paper.

PRINTER'S INK.

For the production of printing ink fast to washing, take 5 parts of acetic acid and dissolve therein 1 part of lunar caustic. Stand away this solution for one day, and add 20 parts of copal varnish, to which a little lampblack is added. Since the brown shade of the lunar caustic coloring predominates after repeated washings, especially if the wash is exposed to the sun, it is advisable to give the print a greenish appearance by moistening it lightly with a few drops of water in which a little potassium iodide has been dissolved. This ink should be used as fresh as possible, and the lunar caustic dissolved in acetic acid and the copal varnish solution should, therefore, each be kept in a closed flask, from which the quantity necessary for the print is taken each time in the said proportion.

PRODUCTION OF DAMASK IN RELIEF UPON GUN-BARRELS.

To produce damask in relief upon gun-barrels, first close with corks all the openings of the barrel and free it from adhesive grease. Next place it in a box pitched inside and pour over it a mixture of 1 qt. water with 1 oz. hydro-chloric acid. Allow the barrel to remain in this mixture for three or four hours, when it is taken from the box, washed with water, rubbed with tow dipped in tripoli and then thoroughly dried. It is next allowed to heat over a coal fire. This treatment causes the steel portions to appear in relief, the iron parts having been subject to attack by corrosive solution.

PROTECTING IRON FROM RUST.

To protect iron from rust, mix fine, pulverized zinc with oil and a dryer. Apply with a common brush. Two applications give a fine steel gray color and perfect protection.

PROTECTING IRON WORK FROM RUSTING.

One-half ounce camphor, 1 pound of lard, and black lead enough to color, is said to protect iron work from rusting.

PRUSSIATE OF SILVER.

Prussiate of silver is prepared by passing cyanogen gas through a cold solution of nitrate of silver.

PULVERIZING SOLDER.

To pulverize solder or block tin, melt the metal, but do not let it get any hotter than barely to liquefy it; pour it out into an old ticking apron, gather up the corners and rub or knead it briskly between the hands, until it is granulated.

PURIFYING CISTERN WATER.

To purify water in cisterns and casks when it has become impure and dirty, for each hogshead of water contained in the cistern or cask sprinkle into it a tablespoonful of pulverized alum, stirring the water at the same time. The impurities will be precipitated to the bottom in a few hours and the water will be found clean and clear.

PURPLE OF CASSIUS.

Purple of Cassius is prepared by the dissolution of 30 86-100 grains of tin in boiling aqua regia, the solution being evaporated at a gentle heat until solid. Next comes its dissolution in distilled water, and after the addition of 30 86-100 grains of stannous chloride solution diluted with 10 quarts of water.

A solution of chloride of gold from 75-100 grains of gold is then stirred into the fluid. On adding 1 ounce 12 drachms of ammonia the fluid becomes turbid and the fluid easily separates out.

PUTTY—STOVE.

For a stove putty use Portland cement. It is not quite as permanent, perhaps, as a rust joint, but for inexperienced persons it is very valuable. It is often used in putting iron pipes together and works well. It is safer in green hands than lead, which has to be well caulked and may fail even when well put in, if exposed to extremes of temperature.

(2) A stove putty which is very good and cheap can be prepared as follows: To every pound of mineral brown, add one ounce of soapstone, and mix with boiled oil.

QUEEN'S METAL.

Queen's Metal is composed of

9-10 parts Zinc,
3 5-10 parts Copper,
7 1-10 parts Antimony,
88 5-10 parts Tin.

RECOVERY OF GOLD AND SILVER FROM SWEEPINGS, ETC.

To recover gold and silver from sweepings and other refuse, dry the latter and heat them in a Hessian crucible. The glowed mass is then to be triturated in an enameled kettle with water and treated with an excess of hydro-chloric acid for the dissolution of any calcium carbonate or alkalies that may be present. The portion as yet undissolved will contain ferric oxide, clay, sand, copper, gold and silver. The silver is recovered from it by washing thoroughly with distilled water, followed by boiling in pure nitric acid, which results in the absorption of the silver by the acid. Next brush the residue and from the combined fluids there is a precipitation of silver and chloride of silver by either hydro-chloric acid or common salt, preferably the former. The residue still undissolved should be heated with aqua regia and the precipitation of the gold will be caused by the addition of copperas. It may be advisable to treat the undissolved residue with ammonia for the extraction of the chloride of silver.

RECOVERY OF NICKEL FROM OLD SOLUTIONS.

To recover nickel from old solutions take ammonium-sulphate in warm water, which is to be constantly stirred into the old nickel-plating solution. After this has been done for a little while the separation of the granular precipitation of the double sulphate of nickel will commence. Continue the addition of the ammonium-sulphate until the liquid is colorless.

RECOVERY OF TIN FROM SCRAP.

To recover tin from tinplate waste or scrap, treat same with dilute chlorine, hotter than chlorine of tin, at the boiling point, so that the latter, directly upon its formation, evaporates, as if it stays in the form of a fluid touching the residues, it effects the formation of chlorine of iron, the reduction of tin taking place. The fumes of chlorine of tin are precipitated by steam, or by contact with moist surfaces in the chambers of condensation, or their absorption by a medium concentrated solution of chlorine of tin takes place. Another way of recovering tin from waste is to bring same into contact with sulphur in a boiling hot solution of sodium-sulphide, which thoroughly frees the iron from tin. This waste, which has been freed from tin, is washed and dried, heated to a welding heat in rolled iron tubs, and is then hammered into rod-iron. Then proceed to the evaporation of solution of sodium-sulphide, which holds the tin and calcine the residue in a reverberatory furnace. After this, reduce the calcine mass to tin at a raised heat by aid of a compound burned lime, charcoal and small coal.

REFRACTORY SOLDER FOR ENAMELED WORK.

A refractory solder for enameled work is made of

18 parts Silver,
74 parts Gold.

REMOVING ACID SPOTS FROM STEEL.

The application of rotten stone and oil will generally remove acid spots from steel. It will also remove rust, and bath brick will give the metal the desired polish. This brilliancy of steel may be retained indefinitely if, after final polishing, it be washed in hot suds and rinsed in clear, hot water.

REMOVING GREASE FROM FILE TEETH.

To remove oil or grease from the teeth of a new file, rub chalk or charcoal on the teeth, and clean with a file card. Repeat the operation until the oil or grease is absorbed and removed.

REMOVING MINERAL OIL OR WAX SPOTS.

For removing mineral oil or wax spots, which are very hard to eradicate, especially when they have penetrated deeply into the fibre, owing to ironing of the said bodies, aniline is recommended. This remedy is used in the following mixture: Aniline, 1 part; soap, 1 part; water, 19 parts.

REMOVING OLD PUTTY.

Any one who has tried to remove old, dry putty from a window will agree that it is far from being a pleasant job. An easy way to accomplish it is to pass a hot iron, as a soldering iron, over the putty, which will soften it so it may be readily removed with a knife or chisel.

REMOVING RUST FROM CAST-IRON.

To remove rust from cast-iron, use the following: To 1 part sulphuric acid add 10 parts water, into which dip the casting. When it is withdrawn it should be at once dipped into hot lime water, and held there until it becomes so heated that it will dry immediately when taken out. Then rub with dry bran or sawdust, and a clean surface is the result.

REMOVING RUST FROM KNIVES.

To remove rust from knives cover them with sweet oil, well rubbed on, and after two days take a lump of fresh lime and rub till the rust disappears.

REMOVING RUST FROM NICKEL-PLATE.

To remove rust stains from nickel-plate grease the rust stains with oil, and after a few days rub thoroughly with a cloth moistened with ammonia. If any spots still remain, remove them with dilute hydrochloric acid and polish with tripoli.

REMOVING RUST FROM POLISHED STEEL.

To remove rust from polished steel articles, soak the rusty places for a few days with oil and then scour with emery or tripoli and oil, using a stick of hard wood. Wipe off the oil and all other impurities; rub the stains once more with emery and wine vinegar, and finally polish with fine bloodstone and leather.

REMOVING RUST FROM STEEL.

Cover the steel thoroughly with sweet oil and let it remain there for about three days. Then take some unslaked lime, finely powdered, and rub with it until all rust disappears.

REMOVING RUST FROM STEEL TOOLS.

Rust may often be removed from steel tools by immersing them in kerosene oil for a few days. This loosens the rust so that it may rub off. Where the rust is not very deep-seated emery paper will do, but if of long standing the tools must be refinished.

REMOVING RUSTY BOLTS.

To remove bolts that are rusted without breaking them, the most effective remedy known is the liberal application of petroleum. Care must be taken that the rusted parts are reached by it, and some time must be allowed to give it a chance to soften the layer of rust, before any attempts are made to remove the bolt. If, before the bolt has been driven, it could be dipped into a mixture of graphite grease, or graphite oil, it would never rust. Graphite prepared in this way, with grease or oil, absolutely prevents rust.

REMOVING STAINS FROM IVORY.

To remove stains from ivory, immerse the pieces in benzine and go over them with a brush.

REMOVING TARNISH FROM GOLD AFTER HARD SOLDERING.

The gold is first protected by a coat of yellow ochre paint and ground up with water to which a small quantity of borax has been added. After the soldering, put same in a pickle composed of 1 part sulphuric acid diluted with 6 parts of water. Should the gold, on emerging from this pickle, look whitish and show too much of the silver alloy, it should be plunged for a moment in a heated mixture of saltpetre and sulphuric acid, to which no water has been added. It should then be washed and polished with rotten stone aid oil. Then comes a second washing and polishing with rouge.

REPAIRING LEAKY GUTTERS.

To repair leaky gutters while constantly filling with water from melting snow and ice, when you cannot bail the water out fast enough to enable you to solder the broken seams: Make a syphon with a ½-inch rubber tube and start it running, and in a few minutes the gutter will be clear of water so the work can be done.

REPAIRING VALLEYS.

To repair on old valley, cut off all but 1½ inches of it and turn up the remaining part. Turn up the new valley 2 inches, turn over the 1½ inch part, mallet down and solder. If too rusty for that, turn the old and new up 1½ inches and 1¼ inches respectively, and double seam.

REPAIRING WRINGERS.

File shaft bright and rough; warm it; also warm the roll, and when warm enough plug up one end and fill with rubber cement. Next apply cement to the shaft with a brush, empty the roll and adjust it to the shaft. The shaft being warm the cement will adhere to it; the roll being warm becomes soft and elastic.

REPAIRING WRINGER ROLLS.

First file the shaft bright, apply a coat of varnish and let it harden, then apply another coat, and, while green, wind with jute twine. Apply two or three coats of thick rubber cement, fasten shaft upright in vise, warm roll to soften it, then give shaft a coat of thin cement, and swab out the roll with the same and slide quickly down to place, and let stand twenty-four hours before using. This will make a job that will stick.

REPLACING BOILER BOTTOMS.

When a boiler is to be "cut down," it must be evident that the first step is to remove the old bottom. The edge can be knocked back and the outer edge removed by cutting off the outer edge of the burr, so that by heating the remainder of the double-seam it can be taken off with a pair of pliers. After this a burr can be turned on the bottom again; of course, it cannot be double-seamed again, but must be slipped on.

ROBIERRES' METAL.

Robierres' metal is a copper-zinc alloy composed of

66 parts Copper,
34 parts Zinc.

ROSEINE.

Roseine is an alloy composed of 40 parts nickel, 10 parts silver, 30 parts aluminum, and 20 parts tin, for jewelers' work.

ROSE'S METAL.

Rose's metal is composed of tin (1 part), lead (1 part), bismuth (2 parts).

ROSTHORNS' STERRO-METAL.

Rosthorns' sterro-metal is a copper-zinc alloy composed of

55 33-100 parts Copper,
41 8-10 parts Zinc,
4 67-100 parts Iron.

ROUGE FOR POLISHING METALS.

A rouge for polishing metals is obtained as follows: Sulphate of iron is to be heated in an iron vessel over a slow fire and continuously stirred with an iron spatula until it becomes dry and assumes the form of a pale, greenish-yellow powder. Crush this powder in a mortar and sift same. Then calcine it in a new crucible and give it an exposure to the fire of a smelting stove, as long as it continues fuming. As soon as vapors cease arising from it the contents of the crucible may be left to cool and then they will look like the rouge employed in the polishing. The color of the resultant rouge may range from pale red to brown-red, or may be blue and violet. These varieties, however, are caused merely by the different degrees of heat employed, and it may be laid down as an axiom that the higher the temperature during the process of manufacture, the darker the color of the powder and the harder it will be. This is also the explanation of the reason why the violet powder is employed for steel, and the pale red powder is only used for silver and gold. Questions of color aside, it is vitally essential that the rouge be well bruised and washed in water before its employment. To do this you take three glasses and fill one of them with clear water, in which a little rouge is mixed by stirring it a minute or two with a little piece of wood. After the rouge has been allowed to settle to the bottom of the glass (the time being about ½ minute) the remainder of the liquid is decanted into the second glass, but every particle of the deposit is to be left in the first one. This identical process is followed for the second and third glasses, but there is this difference: The powder in the second glass is allowed to settle fully two minutes, while the powder in the third glass is left for two or three hours, which is the time required for the assumption by the water of its natural clearness. The sediment in the first glass is of no value; that in the second, of medium quality, while that in the third is very good and can be very advantageously employed after it has been slowly dried. In some cases this rouge may be mixed with grease, and as a general rule found quite advantageous to wet it with spirits of wine and burn it in a clean iron vessel.

ROUGHENING SHEET-BRASS.

To make sheet-brass rough so you can paint on same with oil paint, place it for twelve hours in a pickle consisting of 8 parts water, 1 part concentrated hydro-chlorate acid and 8 parts concentrated sulphuric acid. It is next to be rinsed off with water. If it is desired to hasten the moire-like appearance given by this process, a compound of hydro-chloric acid and potassium bicarbonate may be used and also a galvanic battery.

RUSTED SCREWS—LOOSENING.

To loosen rusted screws, apply heat at the head of the screw and take a small bar of iron, flat at the end, redden it in the fire and apply for two or three minutes to the head of the rusty screw. As soon as the screw is heated, this will make it as easy to take it out with a screwdriver as if it had only recently been inserted.

RUST—FREEING POLISHED STEEL ARTICLES FROM.

To remove rust from polished steel articles the spots affected should be soaked for several days with oil, and then scoured with tripoli and oil, or with emery, a piece of hard wood being used for this purpose. The oil and all other impurities are then to be wiped off. The stains are to to be rubbed a second time with emery and wine vinegar and then polished with fine bloodstone and leather.

RUST—INGRAINED REMOVAL OF IRON FROM.

To thoroughly clean iron from rust, first immerse it in deeply saturated solution of chloride of tin. The length of said bath should be dependent on the thickness of the film of rust. As a general rule, however, from twelve to twenty-four hours will be amply sufficient. Care should be taken that this solution of the chloride of tin should not contain too heavy an assiduous excess, otherwise the iron itself will be attacked. After the removal of the articles from the bath they should first be washed in water followed by a second washing with ammonia, and then dried as rapidly as possible. Articles thus treated primarily assume the appearance of dead silver, but regain their natural appearance by simply polishing.

RUSTING—TO PREVENT METALS FROM.

A good compound to prevent metals from rusting is

made by melting 1 ounce of resin in a gill of linseed oil and mixing it with 2 quarts of kerosene oil while warm.

RUSTING—TO PREVENT STEEL FROM.

To prevent steel from rusting, brush it with a solution of paraffine and benzine.

RUST—TO EXTRACT FROM NICKEL-PLATED ARTICLES.

To free nickel-plated articles from rust, grease the rust stain, and a few days thereafter rub them thoroughly with a cloth wet with ammonia. The dissolution of the rust is effected by the ammonia without harm to the plating. If this method does not work satisfactorily, the stains may be touched with diluted hydro-chloric acid and vigorously rubbed. They should then be washed, and on becoming dry polish with tripoli or some similar polishing material.

RUST—TO EXTRACT FROM STEEL.

To extract rust from steel, plunge the article to be cleaned in a strong solution of cyanide of potassium consisting of ½ ounce in a wineglass of water, for a few minutes, and then take it out and clean with a small brush, such as a toothbrush, dipped into a composition of castile soap, cyanide of potassium, whiting and water made into a paste of about the thickness of ordinary cream.

SCHWEINFURT GREEN.

Schweinfurt green is made by boiling a mixture of

10 6-10 parts Acetic Acid,
31 26-100 parts Cupric Oxide,
58 65-100 parts Arsenious Acid.

It is very poisonous.

SCOURING CAST-IRON, ZINC OR BRASS.

To scour cast-iron, zinc or brass surfaces with great economy of labor, time and material, by using either glycerine, stearine, naphtha, lime or creosote mixed with diluted sulphuric acid.

SCRATCH-BRUSHING.

To brighten articles in relief, scratch-brushes are used oftener than store or steel burnishers. A common scratch-brush is constructed of a large number of hardened brass wires selected from a coil of large diameter, so that there will be little tendency of the wires, when in place, toward curvature. For the manufacture of a good scratch-brush select a coil of brass wire of the right fineness and bind tightly with strong twine of about 2-3 the desired length of the brush, say 6 or 7 inches. Cut the bundle of wire close to the cord at one end, and about 2 inches from the other, with a chisel. The close cut end is to be dipped into a neutral solution of chloride of zinc and plunged into molten tin, which solders all the wires and guards against their separation. This, too, is preferably fixed by means of another string to a thin wooden handle projecting above the soldered end.

SCREWS—TO PREVENT FROM RUSTING.

To prevent screws from rusting in machines and other metal work subject to exposure to moist air or heat, dip them before use in a thin paste consisting of oil of graphite.

SEPARATION OF GOLD FROM GILDED ARTICLES.

To separate gold from gilded metallic articles, dip them in a concentrated solution of sal-ammoniac in vinegar which has been heated to a dark red heat. Then immerse them in dilute sulphuric acid, which will cause the gold to separate in thin scales. If it is desired to obtain the gold in a coherent form, fuse the scales with saltpeter and borax.

SEPARATION OF LEAD FROM ZINC.

You will have great difficulty in separating lead from zinc. If you have the necessary appliances for heating the mass sufficiently the zinc will partially evaporate and leave the lead on being treated. If the whole is granulated the zinc could be dissolved by acids. Zinc being of lighter specific gravity than lead it will float on the latter when properly heated, and to a certain extent can be skimmed off. You will find all these processes troublesome, and in the end not entirely satisfactory.

SEPARATION OF ZINC FROM LEAD.

To separate zinc from lead, melt the alloy and the heavier lead will collect in the lower part of the crucible with the lighter zinc from above. The latter can then be easily poured off.

SEPIA BROWN FOR TIN.

In order to give tin a sepia-bronze appearance, brush the article with the following solution, viz., 1 part of platinum chloride in 10 parts of water. The coating should be allowed to dry, then rinsed in water, again allowed to dry and then brushed with a soft brush until the requisite luster makes its appearance.

SHARPENING FILES.

To sharpen files, a metal sheet covered with a thin layer of charcoal is fastened upon the file, protecting the edges. This combination is laid into a solution of six parts of nitric acid and three parts of sulphuric acid in a hundred parts of water. The acid eats away all the inner parts of the file, leaving the protected edges unchanged, which are then sharpened for use.

SILVER CARBONATE.

Silver carbonate is a precipitation formed by bringing together solutions of nitrate of silver and potash.

SILVER—HORN.

Horn silver is obtained by the addition of hydrochloric acid to a solution of nitrate of silver.

SILVERING BRONZE.

To give a silver color to bronze proceed to the dissolution, in a vessel that is well glazed, of

1½ drachms Tartar Emetic.
1½ ounces Pulverized Cream of Tartar.
in
1 quart Hot Water,

and add to this solution

1 ounce Pulverized Antimony,
1¾ ounces Hydro-chloric Acid.

The articles to be coated are immersed in this solution, which is to be heated to the boiling point and allowed to boil for from 15 to 30 minutes; at the end of this time they will be given a beautiful, lustrous coating.

SILVERING CAST IRON.

A bath prepared by dissolving 3½ drachms nitrate of silver in 7 ounces of water and adding 7 drachms of cyanide of potassium may be used for this purpose. This solution is to be poured into 21 ounces of water, wherein 3½ drachms of common salt have been previously dissolved. The cat-iron intended to be silvered by the solution should, after having been cleaned, be placed for a few minutes in a bath of dilute nitric acid just previous to being placed in the silvering fluid.

SILVERING CAST ZINC.

The dark colors in silvered cast zinc articles are obtained by coating same with a solution of liver of sulphur, and also by rubbing with graphite.

SILVERING IRON.

To silver iron, first cover the iron with mercury, and silver by the galvanic process. By heating 300 degrees C., the mercury evaporates and the silver layer is fixed. Ironware is first heated with diluted hydrochloric acid, and then dipped in a solution of nitrate of mercury, being at the same time in communication with the zinc pole of an electric battery, a piece of gas carbon or platinum being used as an anode for the other pole. The metal is soon covered with a layer of quicksilver: is then taken out and well washed and silvered in a silver solution. To save silver, the ware can first be covered with a layer of tin; one part of cream of tartar is dissolved in eight parts of boiling water, and one or more tin anodes are joined with the carbon pole of a Bunsen element. The zinc pole communicates with a well-cleaned piece of copper, and the battery is made to act till enough tin is deposited on the copper, when this is taken out and the ironware put in its place. The ware thus covered with tin chemically pure and silvered is much cheaper than any other silvered metals.

SILVERING MIRRORS.

In making mirrors, mercury or quicksilver is poured over tin foil and the glass (absolutely clean) carefully slid upon it so as to exclude the air, when weights are placed upon it and allowed to remain several hours. The mercury and tin foil combine and adhere to the glass.

(2) The glass is first silvered by means of tartaric acid and ammoniacal nitrate of silver, and then exposed to the action of a weak solution of double cyanide of mercury and potassium. When the mercurial solution has spread uniformly over the surface, fine zinc dust is powdered over it, which promptly reduces the quicksilver, and permits it to form a white and brilliant amalgam, adhering strongly to the glass, and which is free from the yellowish tint of ordinary silvered glass, and not easily affected by sulphurous emanations.

SILVERING LIGHT—TEST FOR.

To determine whether silvering on an article is light or heavy, clean same with either ether or alcohol and apply to it a drop of 1 5-10 per cent. solution of bisulphate of soda. Allow the drop to act for ten minutes and rinse it off with water. If the article is deeply silvered a full round steel-gray spot is produced. Other white metals, barring amalgamated copper, do not show this, but, instead, a ring at the edge of the drop.

SILVERING SOLUTION—NON-POISONOUS.

Take nitrate silver 2 drachms, distilled water 4½ ounces. Dissolve, and add sal-ammoniac, hyposulphite soda and precipitated chalk each 4 drachms. Mix.

All surfaces to be plated must be thoroughly cleansed and polished before applying the solution.

SILVER INK.

A silver ink may be made by rubbing up silver bronze with honey and water.

SILVER LIQUID—TEST FOR.

To determine whether an article is silver or silvered apply the following test: viz., a fluid consisting of 16 parts chromic acid and 32 parts of distilled water. The surface of the article to be tested is to be filed, and the filed place put on the touch-stone and the test water applied. If genuine silver, the touchstone becomes blood red. The deeper the coloration, the finer the quality of the silver. If the article be not genuine silver, but silvered, German silver, tin compositions, etc., the touch is not decomposed by the test water, but cast out in its original color, or, perhaps, in extreme cases, with a dull gray tint.

SILVEROID.

This alloy is very white and fine-grained, and has great tenacity. It is used in place of brass or gun metal where a superior polish is required and is composed of copper and nickel, to which, according to the different purposes for which it is desired, zinc, lead and tin are added.

SILVER SULPHATE.

Silver sulphate is made by the action of hot, concentrated sulphuric acid on silver.

SILVER SULPHIDE.

Silver sulphide is made by the fusion of silver with sulphur.

SIMILOR.

Similor is a copper-zinc alloy composed of

89 44-100 parts Copper,
9 93-100 parts Zinc,
62-100 parts Tin.

SOAP FOR METAL WORK.

A soap for metal work is as follows: The basis is cocoanut oil. Its ingredients are cocoanut oil, 2.5 kilos; chalk, 180 grms.; and alum, cream of tartar and white lead, of each 87.5 grms. The oil is melted in an iron vessel containing a little water, and the other ingredients are added in the order named, while constantly stirring the mixture. The mixture is then decanted into molds, wherein it solidifies. In use it is made into a paste with water and applied either by cotton waste or a rag. It is said this preparation never spoils in keeping.

SOFTENING CAST-IRON.

To soften cast-iron, steep in 1 part of aqua fortis to 4 parts of water, and let it remain in twenty-four hours.

SOFTENING RUBBER.

To soften rubber: If the rubber is unvulcanized, naphtha, bisulphide of carbon, and a variety of solvents may be employed, or slight heating will make a soft dough of it. If the rubber be vulcanized soft (like the rubber parts of boots and shoes), it cannot be softened without injury to it. Animal oils will do the softening in this case, but destroy the rubber instantly. If the rubber be hard (like penholders, buttons, etc.), it may be softened by heat and its shape changed by pressing. Rubber may be melted, but in every case it is ruined by such treatment, the result being a tar-like fluid that never again regains its original condition.

SOFTENING SOLDERING COPPERS.

To soften soldering coppers that have been hardened by use, heat the soldering coppers red-hot or to a cherry heat, then plunge them into cold water.

SOFTENING STEEL.

For softening steel so that it can be engraved and otherwise worked similarly to copper, pulverize beef bones and mix them with equal parts of calves' hair and loam and stir the mixture into a thick paste with water. A coat of this is applied to the steel and placed in a crucible. This is covered with another; the two are fastened with wire together, and the joint is closed hermetically with clay. The crucible is then placed in the fire and heated slowly. When through heating, it is cooled by being placed in the ashes.

SOLDER.

A soft alloy, which adheres so firmly to metallic, glass and porcelain surfaces that it can be used as solder, and which is invaluable when the articles to be soldered are of such a nature that they cannot bear a high degree of temperature, consists of finely pulverized copper dust, which is obtained by shaking a solution of the sulphate of copper with granulated zinc. The temperature of the solution rises considerably and the metallic copper is precipitated in the form of a brownish powder; 20, 30 or 36 parts of this copper dust, according to the hardness desired, are placed in a cast-iron or porcelain-lined mortar and well mixed with some sulphuric acid having a specific gravity of 185. Add to the paste thus formed 70 parts (by weight) of mercury, constantly stirring. When thoroughly mixed the amalgam must be rinsed in warm water to remove the acid, and then set aside to cool. In ten or twelve hours it will be hard enough to scratch tin. When it is to be used it should be heated to a temperature of 375 degrees C., when it becomes as soft as wax by kneading in an iron mortar. In this ductile state it can be spread upon any surface, to which, as it cools and hardens, it adheres very tenaciously.

(2) A solder for various metals, particularly aluminum, consists in combining cadmium, zinc and tin mixed in substantially the following proportions: Cadmium, 50 per cent.; zinc, 20 per cent.; tin, the remainder. The zinc is first melted in any suitable vessel, when the cadmium is added, and then the tin in pieces. The mass must be well heated, stirred, and then poured.

SOLDER—ACIDS FOR.

To solder galvanized iron, also to solder tin to any iron: Muriatic acid reduced with zinc is used in soldering iron and tin, but it should be wiped off at once. It is used raw or unreduced in soldering galvanized iron.

SOLDER—ARGENTAN.

An Argentan solder, which is readily adapted for use in iron and steel is composed of

12 parts Nickel,
38 parts Copper,
50 parts Zinc.

Another Argentan solder which fuses readily is composed of

8 parts Nickel,
35 parts Copper,
57 parts Zinc.

SOLDER—BISMUTH.

Bismuth solder is composed of the following:

(1) Lead, 4 parts; tin, 4 parts; bismuth, 1 part.
(2) Lead, 3 parts; tin, 3 parts; bismuth, 1 part.
(3) Lead, 2 parts; tin, 2 parts; bismuth, 1 part.
(4) Lead, 2 parts; tin, 1 part; bismuth, 2 parts.
(5) Lead, 3 parts; tin, 5 parts; bismuth, 3 parts.
(6) Bismuth solder is made of 1 part lead and 1

part tin and 1 part bismuth, which melts at 284 degrees Fahrenheit.

SOLDER FOR ALUMINUM.

For sheet aluminum an iron tin solder may be used with a flux composed of resin, neutral chloride of zinc, and grease. The metal should not be cleaned or scraped unless it is absolutely necessary to do so, in which case alcohol or essence of turpentine should be used for the purpose. For 5 per cent. aluminum bronze tin solder may be employed, but this is not possible with the 10 per cent. alloy, in which case the company recommends a preliminary copper plating. If it is difficult to dip the ends to be plated directly into the solution pieces of blotting paper soaked in a solution of $CuSO_4$ may be laid on them and a current passed. The flux mentioned above may be used.

Another solder which is recommended is one consisting of: Copper, 56 parts; zinc, 46 parts, and tin, 2 parts, applied with borax. In a test plates of aluminum soldered together, edge to edge, with these solubles required a tractive effort of 16½ to 18 tons per square inch to pull them asunder; if the edges overlapped, 22¼ tons per square inch were required. Pieces of cast aluminum bronze, if placed in sand molds, can be joined together autogenously by running in some of the molten metal. If this operation is properly carried out the joint is indistinguishable from the rest of the casting. Thin cylinders of aluminum are made in this way by bending the sheets round end to end, and soldering with molten aluminum.

A solder for aluminum consists in combining cadmium, zinc and tin mixed in substantially the following proportions: Cadmium, 50 parts; zinc, 20 parts; tin, the remainder. The zinc is first melted in any suitable vessel, when the cadmium is added and then the tin in pieces. The mass must be well heated, stirred, and then poured. The soldering metal can be used for a variety of different metals, but is specially adapted to aluminum.

SOLDER FOR BRITANNIA METAL.

For Britannia metal a solder is used consisting of 1 part lead and 2 parts tin, with resin or chloride of zinc as a flux. The proportion of soft solder is made by first melting the tin in either a porcelain or stone vessel. After it has been melted the lead is added in small proportions and the combination of the two metals is effected by stirring with a stick of wood. The alloy is then to be poured into molds, one of the best shapes being 7¾ inches long and 1½ inches high and ⅛ to ¼ inch thick.

(2) A solder for Britannia metal is composed as follows: Tin, 8 parts; lead, 4 parts; bismuth, 1 part. Melt at a moderate heat and run into bars.

SOLDER FOR ALUMINUM.

The composition of solders for aluminum that are generally used is as follows:

(1) 80 parts Zinc.
12 parts Aluminum,
8 parts Copper.

(2) 88 parts Zinc.
7 parts Aluminum,
5 parts Copper.

(3) 94 parts Zinc,
4 parts Aluminum.
2 parts Copper.

(4) 90 parts Zinc.
6 parts Aluminum,
4 parts Copper.

(5) 85 parts Zinc,
9 parts Aluminum,
6 parts Copper,

First prepare an aluminum copper alloy which is to be mixed with the requisite amount of zinc. Melt the copper and then gradually introduce into same the aluminum, divided into 3 or 4 portions; make a perfect mixture by stirring. After the last of the aluminum has been put in, throw in the zinc and with it some fat or resin, then stir the mass rapidly and directly remove the crucible from the fire and pour the alloy into iron molds, which have been rubbed with benzine or cold tar oil.

SOLDER FOR ALUMINUM.

A good aluminum solder is made of zinc, aluminum and copper, in the proportion of 90, 6 and 4.

SOLDER FOR ALUMINUM BRONZE JEWELRY.

A solder for aluminum bronze jewelry is composed of

18 per cent. Copper,
27 6-10 per cent. Silver,
50 4-10 per cent. Gold.

(2) A second solution is composed of

6 44-100 per cent. Copper,
4 68-100 per cent. Silver,
88 88-100 per cent. Gold.

SOLDER FOR GERMAN SILVER.

A solder for German silver is composed of the following: German silver, 5 parts; pure zinc, 4 parts. German silver used is made of: Copper, 8 parts; nickel, 2 parts, and zinc, 3.5 parts.

SOLDER FOR GLASS.

To make a good solder for glass make an alloy of 95 per cent. tin and 5 per cent. zinc.

SOLDER FOR GOLD.

The best solder for uniting gold is made by melting 66.6 parts gold with 16.7 copper, and 16.7 silver. This alloy is a firm and easily working solder, though a very good solder for gold for general purposes is made by adding to 100 parts gold, 40 of silver, and 30 of copper.

SOLDER FOR HARD BRASS.

A solder for hard brass is composed of the following: Scraps of metal to be soldered, 4 parts; zinc, 1 part.

SOLDER FOR IRON AND STEEL INSTRUMENTS.

For the finer kinds of iron and steel instruments gold is an excellent solder, as it possesses the power of dissolving iron in a degree of heat far less than is required for melting iron. Therefore, if a small plate of gold is wrapped round the parts to be joined, and then melted with the blow-pipe, it strongly unites the parts together without any injury whatever to the instrument, however delicate.

SOLDER FOR NICKEL.

The following has proved a good formula for making solder for nickel: For fine or high-grade nickel, 3 parts yellow brass, 1 part coin silver. For low-grade nickel, 15 parts yellow brass, 5 parts coin silver, 4 parts zinc (pure or plate zinc). Melt the brass and copper with borax for a flux, and add the zinc in small pieces, stir with an iron rod, pour in a slab mold, and cool slowly, when it can be rolled thin for cutting.

SOLDER FOR SILVER.

Among the common hard silver solders for first soldering are those made in the following proportions:

(1)	10	parts	Brass,
	5	parts	Zinc,
	1	part	Copper,
	19	parts	Fine Silver.
(2)	3	parts	Brass,
	4	parts	Fine Silver.
(3)	1	part	Brass,
	2	parts	Fine Silver.

(4) 16 6-10 parts Zinc,
33 4-10 parts Copper,
50 parts Fine Silver.

(5) 11 parts Zinc,
25 7-10 parts Copper,
66 3-10 parts Fine Silver.

(6) 10 parts Zinc,
23 3-10 parts Copper,
66 7-10 parts Fine Silver.

(7) 35 parts Zinc,
157 parts Brass,
9 parts Fine Silver.

(8) 18 parts Zinc,
76 parts Brass,
6 parts Fine Silver.

(9) 1 part Zinc,
4 parts Brass,
11 parts Fine Silver.

(10) 1 part Zinc,
15 parts Brass,
16 parts Fine Silver.

A softer hard silver solder for after-soldering is variously composed as follows:

(1) 2 6-10 parts Copper,
1 part Zinc,
3 5-10 parts Medium-grade Silver.

(2) 4 5-10 parts Copper,
3 5-10 parts Zinc,
10 5-10 parts Medium-fine Silver.

(3) 3 3-10 parts Tin,
32 3-16 parts Copper,
16 1-10 parts Zinc,
48 3-10 parts Medium-grade Silver.

(4) 1 part Zinc,
7 parts Medium-grade Silver.

(5) 1 part Zinc,
16 parts Medium-grade Silver.

(6) 24 4-10 parts Copper,
10 5-10 parts Zinc,
67 1-10 parts Medium-grade Silver.

(7) 3 parts Copper,
1 part Zinc,
2 parts Medium-grade Silver.

(8) 2 3-10 parts Copper,
8 2-10 parts Zinc,
68 8-10 parts Medium-grade Silver.

SOLDER FOR TIN PANS.

For tin pipes a solder is used consisting of 1 part of lead and 2 parts of tin, which has been used for a compound of sweet oil and resin as a flux.

SOLDER FOR UNITING BRASS TUBE SEAMS.

A solder for uniting brass tube seams is composed of the following: Brass, 77.5 parts; zinc, 22.5. The brass is made as follows: Copper, 70 parts; tin, 30 parts.

SOLDER FOR ZINC CASTINGS.

A good solder for uniting zinc castings, according to Averman, is composed of 2 parts of tin and 1 of zinc. The surfaces to be united are freed from oxide preparatory to using the solder, by the application of either muriatic acid or chloride of zinc.

SOLDER—GOLD.

Gold solder is composed of: Gold, 12 parts; silver, 2 parts; copper, 4 parts.

SOLDER—HARD, FOR COPPER, BRASS AND IRON.

(1) Hard solder for copper, brass and iron, is composed of the following: Copper, 2 parts; zinc, 1 part.

(2) Good tough brass, 5 parts; zinc, 1 part.

(3) More fusible than 1 or 2: Copper, 1 part; zinc, 1 part.

(4) Good tough plate brass.

SOLDER—HARD, FOR GOLD.

Hard solder for gold is composed of the following: Gold (18 karats, or 750-1000), 18 parts; silver, 10 parts; pure copper, 10 parts.

SOLDER—HARD, FOR IRON.

A hard solder for iron is composed of the following: Copper, 67 parts; zinc, 33 parts.

SOLDER—HARD, FOR PURE COPPER OR ORDINARY BRASS.

A hard solder for pure copper or ordinary brass is composed of the following: Copper, 3 parts; zinc, 1 part.

SOLDER—HARD, FOR SILVER.

A hard solder for silver is composed of the following: Silver, 66 parts; copper, 23 parts; zinc, 10 parts.

SOLDER—HARD, FOR SMALL AND THIN PIECES.

A hard solder for small and thin pieces is composed of the following: Copper, 86.5 parts; zinc, 4.5 parts.

SOLDERING ALUMINUM BRONZE.

For soldering aluminum bronze with common soft solder, first thoroughly clean the pieces of bronze from dirt and grease and then put them in a strong solution of sulplate of copper and a rod of soft iron touching the parts to be joined is to be put in the bath. Shortly a copper-like surface will appear on the metal. The pieces of aluminum bronze are then to be removed from the bath, rinsed, cleaned and the surfaces brightened. The surfaces can next be tinged by the use of a fluid made by the dissolution of zinc in hydro-chloric acid.

HULOT'S SOLDER FOR ALUMINUM BRONZE.

Hulot's solder for aluminum bronze is made by compounding solder made of 50 per cent. tin with 12½ per cent., 20 per cent. or 50 per cent. of zinc amalgam.

SOLDERING ALUMINUM WITH A BLOW-PIPE.

To solder aluminum with a blow-pipe, use a compound consisting of

10 parts Copper,
20 parts Aluminum,
60 parts Tin,
10 parts Silver,
30 parts Zinc.

SOLDERING ALUMINUM WITH A SOLDERING-IRON.

To solder aluminum with a soldering-iron use a flux consisting of

97 parts Tin,
3 parts Bismuth,
or
95 parts Tin,
5 parts Bismuth.

The flux to be employed can be either stearin, vaseline or paraffine. Care should be taken that the articles are thoroughly cleaned before they are soldered, and they should be heated just sufficiently to make the adherence of the solder certain.

SOLDERING—AUTOGENOUS.

Autogenous soldering is accomplished by the fusion of the edges of the two metallic articles without the employment of another metallic alloy as a band of union. This is done by the direction of a jet of burning hydro-gas from a little movable beak, upon the two edges or surfaces which it is desired to solder together. There is less liability of metals thus joined cracking asunder at the line of union from strain, temperature, etc., than when the ordinary solder process is used. This system of soldering is quite advantageous in chemical establishments for joining the edges of sheet-zinc for concentrated pans and sulphuric acid chambers, as the speedy corrosion of soldering containing tin is inevitable.

SOLDERING BRASS TO CAST-IRON.

When it is necessary to solder brass to cast-iron, the part of the iron to be soldered should be polished on an emery wheel until it becomes clean and bright. It should then be dipped in potash water, after which it is filtered for a moment in clean water and washed rapidly with ordinary undiluted hydro-chloric acid. It is then gone over with powdered resin and a solder made of 50 per cent. lead and 50 per cent. tin. This step must be taken before the surface drys.

(2) Another method is to file the surface clean, wash same and wipe it with a flux made by the dissolution of sheet-zinc in hydro-chloric acid until the latter is surcharged. That is, when it becomes a saturated solution and has been diluted with its own quantity of water. Then powdered sal-ammoniac is to be sprinkled on it and the mass is to be heated on a charcoal fire until the sal-ammoniac commences to smoke. It is then to be dipped in melted tin and on its removal the surplus tin is to be knocked off.

SOLDERING BRIGHT COPPER.

When it is desired to solder bright copper and to have the solder the same color as the copper surface, it may be done this way: Moisten the solder with a saturated solution of vitriol of copper and then, touching the solder with an iron or steel wire, a thin skin of copper is precipitated, which can be thickened by repeating the process several times.

To make the solder brass-colored, if it is desired to gild the soldered spot, it is first coated with copper in the manner indicated above, and then with gum or isinglass and powdered with bronze powder. The surface thus obtained may, after drying, be brightly polished.

SOLDERING CAST-IRON ARTICLES.

To solder together cast-iron articles, first clean same and then brush with a scratch-brush until they are covered with a dry coat of brass, imparted by said brush. The surface thus covered with brass is then tinned just as brass itself is tinned and the parts are soldered as customary.

SOLDERING ENAMELED WORK.

A fusible solder for enameled work is made from
9 parts Silver,
3 parts Copper,
32 parts Gold (of 750 degrees fineness).

SOLDERING FAT.

To make soldering fat, there should be melted in a pot over a hard coal fire 1 lb. tallow and 1 lb. olive oil, into which is stirred 8 ounces of pulverized colophony and the mass allowed to boil. After the mixture is cooled, add, with constant stirring, ¼ pint of water which has been saturated with pulverized ammonia.

SOLDERING FLUID.

A soft soldering fluid that will not rust tools is found in oleic acid (crude).

(2) For soldering fluid take one drachm each of powdered copperas, borax, and prussiate of potash; ½ ounce of powdered sal-ammoniac; 3½ ounces fluid muriatic acid; let the mixture cut all the zinc it will and then dilute with 1 pint of water.

(3) For soldering fluid: Add granulated zinc or zinc scraps to two fluid ounces of muriatic acid until hydrogen ceases to be given off; add one teaspoonful of ammonium chloride; shake well and add 2 fluid ounces of water.

SOLDERING GRAY CAST-IRON.

To solder gray cast-iron, first dip the castings in alcohol, after which sprinkle muriate of ammonia over the surface to be soldered. Then hold the castings over a charcoal fire till the sal-ammoniac begins to smoke; then dip it into melted tin. This prepares the castings for soldering, which is done in the usual way.

SOLDERING GOLD.

Some of the common soldering for gold is composed of the following ingredients:

1 part Copper,
9 parts Gold,
2 parts Silver.

(This solder is to be used for gold of fineness 750 for hard soldering.)

3 parts Copper,
7 parts Silver,
12 parts Gold.

(This solder is to be used for soft soldering for gold of fineness 750).

(1) 1 part Copper,
2 parts Copper,
3 parts Gold.

(2) 5-10 parts Copper,
5-10 parts Silver,
2 parts Gold.

(These solders are to be used for gold of fineness 583).

(1) 1 part Copper,
2 parts Silver,
1 part Gold.

(2) 2 parts Silver,
1 part Gold.

(3) 2 parts Copper,
1 part Gold.

(These solders are for gold for less fineness than 583).

A solder for gold that is readily fusible consists of

5 1-100 parts Zinc,
54 74-100 parts Silver,
28 17-100 parts Copper,
11 94-100 parts Gold.

SOLDERING LIQUID.

A soldering liquid is prepared by the dissolution of small pieces of zinc in pure hydro-chloric acid until effervescence stops. After a wait of a day or two the undissolved zinc is to be taken out and the solution filtered, compounded with 1-3 its volume of spirits of sal-ammoniac, and then diluted with rain water. If this soldering liquid be used there is no rust caused on iron or steel.

(2) Another soldering liquid is made by the dissolution of 1 part glycerine and 1 part of lactic acid in 8 parts of water.

SOLDERING PASTE.

A soldering paste is made by a mixture of chloride of tin with starch paste.

SOLDERING RUSSIA IRON.

To solder Russia iron, heat the piece of iron with a well-heated soldering iron for about half an inch. It don't want to be made too hot, but draw the iron over same, say for 8 or 10 inches, and then, while it is hot apply raw muriatic acid, rubbing the soldering over same; then with a wet cloth wipe clean and apply cut acid and solder, rubbing the hot iron over same and while hot wipe off with the wet cloth, and it should be as bright as tin and as easy to solder.

SOLDERING SAWS.

To solder saws the tools required are a blow-pipe, a piece of charcoal, some borax and spelter. The ends of the saw are filed smooth, so that one side will lap over the other and the sides opposite each other are to be fitted together and the bundle bound with iron and wire for keeping it in place. The lap is then dampened with borax which has been dissolved in water, and the saw is placed on the charcoal. The broken parts are to be put near the gas-jet and the parts previously wet with the spelter are to be sprinkled and the flame of the gas is to be blown until the spelter runs. It should be cold before it is removed. When quite cold it should be filed quite flat with the other part of the saw.

SOLDERING WITHOUT A SOLDERING-IRON.

For soldering without a soldering-iron, use a fine solder composed of

1 part Tin,
2 parts Bismuth,
2 parts Lead.

Next solder a piece with solder composed of

4 parts Tin,
4 parts Lead,
1 part Bismuth.

The best soldering liquid to employ is made of equal parts of water and hydro-chloric acid which has been saturated with zinc.

SOLDER—PLATINUM.

Platinum crucibles and wires may be soldered by means of fine gold wire in the oxyhydrogen jet. It can also be soldered over a blow-pipe. The solder used is auric chloride (Au Cl), which on heating decomposes first into aurous chloride, and at a higher temperature into chloride and gold. The salt melts at about 200 degrees Cent., and in the blow-pipe the gold runs as a solder. Care should be taken to draw the platinum from the flame when the gold is seen to run, in case it spreads too far and leaves the joint weak. The latter must not afterwards be exposed to a higher temperature than that at which the soldering was effected. In the case of soldered-up longish holes, a spongy platinum may be mixed with the auric acid. Hammering the soldered joint while hot serves to finish off the joint. Wires and strips of platinum can in this way be joined by putting the chloride crystals on each clean surface and gently heating them till nearly black, then binding the surfaces together and further heating them in the blow-pipe fire.

SOLDER—PEWTERERS'.

The coarse solder used by pewterers is formed of tin, 3 parts; lead, 4; and bismuth, 2; the fine, of tin, 2; lead, 1; bismuth, 1.

SOLDER—PLUMBERS' COARSE.

Plumbers' coarse solder is composed of the following: Tin, 1 part; lead, 3 parts.

SOLDER—PLUMBERS' FINE.

Plumbers' fine solder is composed of the following: Tin, 1 part; lead, 2 parts.

SOLDER—PLUMBERS' SEALED.

Plumbers' sealed solder is composed of the following: Tin, 1 part; lead, 2 parts.

SOLDER—SILVER.

To make good, hard silver solder, take 3 parts sterling silver and 1 part brass wire. Melt in a crucible.

The best flux for use with silver solder is borax. Silver solder may be melted in fire or with the use of a blow-pipe.

SOLDER—SILVER, FOR JEWELERS.

Silver solder for jewelers is composed of the following: Silver, 19 parts; copper, 1 part; brass, 1 part.

SOLDER—SILVER, FOR PLATING.

Silver solder for plating is composed of: Silver, 2 parts; copper, 1 part; brass, 1 part.

SOLDER—SILVER, FOR SILVER, BRASS AND IRON.

Silver solder for silver, brass and iron is composed of the following: Silver, 1 part; brass, 1 part.

SOLDER—SILVER, FOR STEEL JOINTS.

Silver solder for steel joints is composed of the following: Silver, 19 parts; copper, 1 part; brass, 1 part.

(2) More fusible: Silver, 5 parts; brass, 5 parts; zinc, 5 parts.

SOLDER—SOFT.

The commonest soft solder used consists of 1 part of lead and 2 parts of tin. The greater the proportion of lead the cheaper will be the solder. The most fusible solder not containing bismuth is made of 1 part of lead and 1½ parts of tin. For ordinary plumbing-work, solders are used composed of

(1)	3	parts	Lead,
	1	part	Tin.
(2)	2	parts	Lead,
	1	part	Tin.
(3)	1	part	Lead,
	1	part	Tin.
(4)	1	part	Lead,
	1½	parts	Tin.
(5)	1	part	Lead,
	2	parts	Tin.

(2) To prepare a soft solder which can be used without acid or a soldering iron, soldering articles of tinware by simply holding over a candle. It is made by melting and mixing 40 parts of tin, 20 parts of lead, 40 parts bismuth by weight, and run into small bars by pouring from a perforated ladle while drawing the ladle across a flat piece of iron, stone or board.

(3) Is composed of 6 parts of lead, 1 part of cadmium, 7 parts of bismuth. Another soft solder is composed of 2 part of lead, 4 parts of tin, and 2 parts of cadmium.

SOLDER—SOFT, FOR ALUMINUM BRONZE.

A soft solder for aluminum bronze is composed of

57 1-10 per cent. Silver.
14 3-10 per cent. Copper.
14 3-10 per cent. Gold,
14 3-10 per cent. Brass.

The brass should be made of

70 per cent. Copper,
30 per cent. Tin.

SOLDER—SPELTER.

Spelter solder is made from equal parts of zinc and copper. When used for brazing the parts should be heated red-hot in a crucible with a flux of borax and charcoal dust, and the addition of the zinc should be made.

(2) Solder of hard spelter (from spelter, the commercial name given to plates of manufactured zinc) is used for joining copper, and is prepared from copper (16 parts) and zinc (12 parts). For soldering brass this formula is changed to one of equal parts copper and zinc, forming the solder known as soft spelter.

SOLDER—TINNERS'.

Tinners' solder is composed of the following: Tin, 1½ parts; lead, 1 part.

SOLDER—TINNERS' FINE.

Tinners' fine solder is composed of the following: Tin, 2 parts; lead, 1 part.

SOLDER—WIRE.

Wire solder, such as is sold to housewives to be used by melting it with a candle, is made as follows: Make a small hole in the bottom of any tin vessel, and allow melted solder to flow through this aperture, while moving the vessel along over an iron surface. Most of the stuff sold by peddlers contains bismuth, and is deleterious when used on culinary utensils.

SPECULUM METAL.

This alloy, commonly used for the manufacture of metallic reflectors, is white in color, and has a hard surface not easily scratched or tarnished. It contains from 64 to 69 per cent. of copper and 30 to 35 per cent. of tin. The white color is made more conspicuous by the addition of small quantities of arsenic and antimony.

STAINING WOOD BLACK.

Almost any wood can be dyed black by the following means: Take logwood extract, powder 1 ounce and boil it in 3¼ pints of water; when the extract is dissolved, add 1 drachm potash yellow chromate (not the bichromate), and agitate the whole. The liquid will serve equally well to write with or to stain wood. Its color is a very fine dark purple, which becomes a pure black when applied to the wood.

STANNIC SULPHIDE.

Stannic sulphide is obtained by passing through a heated tube sulphurated hydrogen and stannic chloride. It can also be made by heating mixtures of corrosive sublimate and stannic sulphide.

STEAM BOILER INSULATION.

To insulate steam boilers, grind with water into a paste of consistency of mortar, asbestos, gypsum, cement and cork waste, applying same with a trowel.

STEEL-GRAY COATING.

The mixture for steel-gray coating is prepared as follows: Triturate 3 85-100 grains of lamp-black with 3 drops of gold-size oil in a dish to a homogeneous cohering mass and dilute this with 24 drops of oil of turpentine. Apply with fine brush in very thin and uniform layers and allow to dry thoroughly.

STEEL-GRAY ON BRASS.

To obtain steel-gray coloring on brass employ a compound of

1 pound Strong Hydro-Chloric Acid,
1 pint of Water,

to which the addition is made of

5¼ ounces Pulverized Antimonic Sulphide,
5¾ ounces Pulverized Iron Filings.

(2) Another mixture for this purpose is composed of hydro-chloric acid compounded with arsenious acid. This compound is put in a lead vessel and the objects immersed in it should be brought in touch with the leaden sides of the vessel or should be enwrapped with a strip of lead.

STEEL-GRAY ON COPPER.

In order to give copper a steel-gray color the articles are to be cleaned and pickled in a heated solution of chloride of antimony in hydro-chloric acid. By the use of a strong galvanic current a coating with a steel-gray precipitation of arsenic may be given the articles by putting them in a heated arsenic bath. If it is desired to give copper a dark, steel-gray color a good pickle consists of 1 quart of hydro-chloric acid, ⅛ quart nitric acid, 1½ ounces iron filings, 1½ ounces arsenious acid.

STEEL MADE TO IMITATE GOLD.

In order to give a ground steel object the appearance of gold or good bronze, the first step is in removing all dirt from the same by a bath in benzine, petroleum or turpentine. It is then to be heated and a light gold varnish applied, which on drying is to be coated with the best copal lacquer.

STERRO-METAL.

Sterro-metal is composed of

54 parts Copper,
40 parts Zinc,
6 parts Ferro-manganese.

TALMI GOLD.

Talmi gold is a copper-zinc alloy composed of

86 4-10 parts Copper,
12 2-10 parts Zinc,
1 1-10 parts Tin,
1 3-10 parts Iron.

TARTAR EMETIC.

Tartar emetic is made by boiling cream of tartar with tetroxide of antimony until its dissolution.

TEMPERING MAGNETS.

To temper magnets, use a water-tight vessel, with two soft-iron pole pieces at the bottom. Place underneath these the poles and electro-magnet. Partially fill the vessel with water, and put a layer of oil above this. Plunge the red-hot bar through these. It will be found that its prior passage through the oil will soften the steel without demagnetization.

TEMPERING MINING PICKS.

To temper mining picks heat them in charcoal fire until red-hot and then immerse in cold rain water and keep there until nearly cold. The use of salt water for this tempering, as is done by many blacksmiths, is erroneous, as there should be no salt in the water, but the same should be cold. If the water is warm, put in a little ice.

TESTING KEROSENE.

The causes of the lamp explosions so frequently reported is the use of poor oil. A simple plan for testing the flashing point of kerosene oil used for illumination is as follows: No kerosene is fit for use in lamps which flashes at a temperature less than 110 degrees Fahr. To test oil, fill a tumbler full of water at 110 degrees Fahr., stir in a tablespoonful of kerosene, and leave until the oil reaches the same temperature. Pass a lighted match over the oil as it floats on the surface, and, if the oil does not ignite it may be safely used. If it flashes at that temperature discard it.

TESTING RUSSIA IRON.

A simple, practical way for testing Russia iron, so as to distinguish readily between the genuine article and the inferior imitations that are in the market: The genuine article is known by its fine black lustre and small granulation of the surface in reflected light. Otherwise by its toughness in bending with and across the grain.

TIERS' ARGENT.

Tiers' argent is an alloy composed of

66 66-100 parts Aluminum,
33 33-100 parts Silver.

TIN—BURNING.

The metal tin can be burned as easily as paper, and to do it makes an interesting parlor experiment. A candle, blow-pipe and tin foil are necessary. With the blow-pipe direct the flame of the candle against a strip of tin foil, and it will readily take fire and burn with a brilliant light, the melted incandescent globules falling to the table and dancing about in a very curious manner. It will be noticed that the product of the combustion of the tin is a white powder, the oxide of tin, and it was observed many years ago that this calx, as it was called, weighed more than the original tin.

TIN FOIL—TESTING.

To discover if an article is tin foil or lead foil plunge

same in a bath of concentrated sulphuric acid. This will dissolve tin, while lead will remain undissolved.

TINNING BATH FOR METALS.

To cover metals with a layer of tin by an immersion process, they are dipped, after being well cleaned, in a boiling bath, containing ammoniacal alum, 535 parts; water, 870 parts; proto-chloride of tin, 31 parts.

(2) Another bath for tinning is the following: Bitartrate of potash, 435 parts; water, 870 parts; proto-chloride of tin, 31 parts.

(3) To cover metals with a layer of tin by means of electricity, the following bath is prepared: Pyrophosphate of potash, 400 parts; proto-chloride of tin, 150 parts; water, 560 parts. The anode is an ingot of pure tin (Banca); the negative is a zinc.

(4) A bath is prepared by leading chlorine through a concentrated solution of chloride of tin until saturated. The excess of chlorine is then driven away by heating the solution after adding to it ten times its volume of water and filtering. The pieces which have to be tinned are cleaned in dilute acid, polished with fine sand, washed, and then, suspended to zinc wire, are left for ten or fifteen minutes in the galvanizing bath. This method has the advantage that the bath becomes charged with chloride of zinc very soon, and that the tin salt must be often added.

(5) Tartaric acid, 62 parts; water, 3,000 parts; soda, 90 parts; proto-chloride of tin, 90 parts.

TINNING.

For putting a thin coat of tin on common black iron, for cold tinning, the following is recommended: Dissolve block tin in muriatic acid and add a little mercury, or one part of tin, two of zinc and six parts of quicksilver. Mix tin and mercury together until they form a paste. Clean the plate, carefully removing all grease, then rub with a piece of cloth moistened with muriatic acid and immediately apply a little of the amalgam to the surface, rubbing it with the same rag.

TINNING BAND IRON.

To tin band iron make a tinning bath as follows: Dissolve with the aid of heat, in an enameled cast-iron kettle, ammonical alum, 11 oz., and fused proto-chloride of tin 1-3 oz. in 4½ gallons of soft water. Clean and rinse the iron to be tinned in cold water, and immerse in the solution as soon as it boils. This process will give a thin coating of tin of a dead lustre, which may be rendered bright by friction. The bath should be maintained at proper length by small additions of proto-chloride of tin.

TINNING BRASS AND COPPER VESSELS.

For tinning brass and copper vessels: The plates or vessels of brass or copper boiled with a solution of stannate of potassia, mixed with turnings of tin, become, in the course of a few minutes, covered with a firmly attached layer of pure tin. (2) A similar effect is produced by boiling the articles with tin-filings and caustic alkali, or cream of tartar. In this way chemical vessels made of copper or brass may be easily and perfectly tinned.

TINNING CAST-IRON.

Have your metal clean, by first scouring, and then swabbing out with dilute acid. Then heat it, and with a wisp of greasy tow rub the molten tin all over. In the dipping process all you have to do is to get the pieces quite clean, and then immerse in a tank of oil or tallow, and when hot pass into the tank of molten tin.

TINNING CAST-IRON STUDS AND CHAPLETS.

Pickle the studs in oil of vitriol, then cover or immerse them in muriate of zinc, after which dip them in a melted bath of tin or solder.

TINNING CLOTH.

To tin cloth, a mixture of finely pulverized metallic zinc and albumen, of about the consistency of thin paste, is spread with a brush upon linen or cotton cloth, and by means of hot steam coagulated. The cloth is now immersed in a bath of stannic chloride, well washed and dried. Running the cloth through a roller press, the tin film is said to take metallic lustre. Designs cut in stout paper, letters, numbers, etc., when laid between cloth and roller, are impressed upon it. It can also be cut in strips, corners, etc.

TINNING METALS.

To cover metals with a layer of tin by an immersion process, they are dipped, after being well cleaned, in a boiling bath containing ammoniacal alum, 535 parts; boiling water, 4,600 parts; proto-chloride of tin, 31 parts. Another bath for tinning is the following: Bitartrate of potash, 435 parts; water, 870 parts; proto-chloride of tin, 31 parts. To cover metals with a layer of tin by means of electricity, the following bath is prepared: Pyro-phosphate of potash, 400 parts; proto-chloride of tin, 150 parts; water, 560 parts. The anode is an ingot of pure tin (Banca); the negative is a zinc ingot.

(2) A bath is prepared by leading chlorine of tin until saturated. The excess of chlorine is then driven away by heating the solution after adding it to ten times its volume of water and filtering. The pieces which have to be tinned are cleaned in dilute acid, polished with fine sand, and then, suspended to zinc wire, are left for ten to fifteen minutes in the galvanizing bath. This method has the inconvenience that the bath becomes charged with chloride of zinc very soon, and that the tin salt must be often added.

(3) Tartaric acid, 62 parts; water, 3,000 parts; soda, 90 parts; proto-chloride of tin, 90 parts.

TINNING SMALL ARTICLES.

To tin small articles, dissolve as much zinc scraps in muriatic acid as it will take up, let it settle, then decant the clear and it is ready for use. Next prepare a suitable iron vessel, set it over the fire, put your tin therein, and melt it, and put as much mutton or beef tallow as will cover the tin about one-fourth inch thick. This prevents the oxidation of the metal; but be careful that the tallow does not catch fire. The iron, or any other metal to be tinned, must be well cleaned, either with scraping, filing, polishing with sand, or immersed in diluted vitriol. Proceed to wet the articles in the zinc solution, then carefully immerse them in the tallow and melted tin; in a very short time they will become perfectly tinned, when they may be taken out.

TINNING SMALL STEEL ARTICLES.

Clean articles bright with sulphuric acid. Having made all parts clean, wash in a solution of sal-ammonia, and dry them in sawdust or by heat; but be sure they are dry before bathing in metal or the metal will fly. You next require a large pot (a glue pot is just the thing), with two compartments, the inner one being perforated to hold the articles to be tinned and the outside one for the metal. Powder your articles with sal-ammoniac and dip them in the molten metal, which should be free from dross; after all smoke has disappeared, lift the inner compartment out, i. e., the one that contains the articles, and sprinkle some more sal-ammoniac over them, also a little over the molten metal, this preventing them from being coated too heavily. When you have reached the same heat as the metal, take them out and shake well to get surplus solder off and cool rapidly in water, drying in sawdust to preserve their lustre. Very small articles can be tinned with a soldering iron and brushed off with a brush, but whichever way is adopted care should be taken to have the articles perfectly clean before starting, and be sure that you get the articles good and hot or the coating of metal will peel off when cold.

TINNING SOLDERING IRONS.

Heat the copper red-hot and file it; have on hand a

piece of sal-ammoniac and rub the copper upon it; then put on a little solder.

TIN PIPE--TESTING FOR LEAD.

To test tin pipe to find whether there is any lead there or not, proceed as follows: On the tinned surface place some string nitric acid, and with a splinter of wood rub it over the surface as large as a 25-cent piece; allow it to dry; when dry two drops of a solution of bi-chromate of potassium should be dropped on the same place. If the tin contains lead, a bright yellow crust of chromate of lead will form on the spot. The test is a very simple one, yet thoroughly reliable, and is decisive.

TIN PUTTY.

Tin putty from glowing oxalate of tin, which is a product of the decomposition of tin-salt with oxalic acid.

TIN SALT.

Tin salt is made by the dissolution of granulated tin in hot hydro-chloric acid, the solution being evaporated to a syrupy consistency and then crystallized.

TIN--TEST FOR.

To test tin, break it, and it will give out a singular crackling sound. Various impurities in tin can be recognized in the following manner: Dissolve tin in clear regia and mix a portion of this solution with potassium ferro-cyanide. If there is a white precipitation, it is tin; if a blue precipitation, there is a trace of iron present; and if there is a red-brown precipitation, there is copper present. For the detection of lead, add to your mixture a quantity of sulphuric acid. To detect the presence of lead in tin dissolve potassium bichromate in water, then acetic acid is to be applied to the tin you wish to test. This will product a whitish coating. Next apply your potassium bichromate solution, and if the whiting coating shows traces of yellow, there is lead in the tin. The yellower the coating, the more lead.

TISSIER'S METAL.

Tissier's metal is a copper-zinc alloy composed of

96 parts Copper,
2 parts Zinc,
1 part Arsenic.

TOMBAC.

Tombac is a copper-zinc alloy composed of

(1) 85 parts Copper,
15 parts Tin.

(2) 92 parts Copper,
8 parts Tin.

(3) 85 3-10 parts Copper,
14 7-10 parts Tin.

(4) 86 4-10 parts Copper,
13 6-10 parts Zinc.

(5) 87 parts Copper,
13 parts Zinc.

(6) 80 parts Copper,
17 parts Zinc,
3 parts Tin.

TOURNAY'S METAL.

Tournay's metal is a copper-zinc alloy composed of

82 54-100 parts Copper,
17 46-100 parts Zinc.

TRACING PAPER.

For ordinary draughtsmen's tracing paper, saturate the paper well with a mixture of one part of balsam of fir and three parts spirits of turpentine. Dry the paper by hanging it up.

(2) A temporarily transparent tracing paper may be made by dissolving castor oil in absolute alcohol, and applying the liquid to the paper with a sponge.

The alcohol evaporates and leaves the paper dry, when the tracing may be made. If the paper is then immersed in absolute alcohol the oil will be removed and the paper restored to its original opacity.

TRANSFER COMPOSITION.

For a transfer composition for transferring figures of any kind on stove patterns: The composition is made of 1½ lbs. dark glue, 1½ lbs. dark resin, 3 lbs. common whiting, 3 gills boiled linseed oil. Dissolving the glue to a thick paste, dissolve the resin in the oil by heating it, mix the whole with the whiting to a heavy dough. Keep the composition in a damp place, and, when desired for use, soften with steam. To transfer ornaments, etc., the first step is to get the ornament or letter sunk in rosewood by a practical stove pattern carver, then press the composition into the die under a light book press (letter press) and a sharp raised transfer of the die is obtained. Cut this off with a knife and paste on the wood pattern with shellac. Artistic ornaments and the entire alphabet will be done to order by a first-class die sinker at a reasonable price.

TRANSFER PAPER FOR METALLIC PATTERNS.

A transfer paper for copying metallic patterns or monumental inscriptions may be made by rubbing a mixture of black lead and soap over the surface of silver paper.

TRIPOLI.

The tripoli which is used for polishing of soft metals, being used first with oil and then dried, is a yellow powder which consists almost entirely of the abundant shells of microscopic organisms.

TUTANIA.

Tutania is composed of

7 6-10 parts Lead,
3-10 parts Zinc,
7-10 parts Copper,
91 4-10 parts Tin.

UNGILDING COPPER.

To ungild copper, which is unable to stand glowing, the gold can be dissolved by being dipped in a warm mixture of 2 64-100 ounces of concentrated hydrochloric acid, 1 pound fuming sulphuric acid, and 1 3-10 ounces of nitric acid of 40 degrees Be. Before these articles are treated in this bath they should be perfectly dry, and the bath itself should not be diluted with water, in which case the acid would act upon the base metals.

UNGILDING IRON AND STEEL.

To remove the gilding from articles of iron and steel they should be given treatment as the anode in a solution of from 2 to 2¾ oz. of 98 per cent. potassium-cyanide in 1 qt. of water and held over a copper-plate, greased with tallow or oil as the cathode.

UNGILDING SILVERWARE.

To remove the gilding from silverware heat same until it glows, and then plunge in diluted sulphuric acid, which will cause the layer of gold to peel off. This process is to be repeated until the removal of all the gold. Prior to the glowing and immersion, the articles may be given a coat of a paste composed of flour of sulphur, sal-ammonium, potassium, nitrate of borax, this paste being allowed to dry. The gold in the gilding will be found on the bottom of the vessel holding the boiled sulphuric acid in the form of scales and laminae. Boil these scales and laminae with pure sulphuric acid, wash them, followed by their dissolution in aqua regia, and make them into chloride of gold or fulminating gold.

UNTINNING OF TINPLATE SCRAPS.

For untinning tinplate scraps, use a large pot containing soda, lye, and oxide of lead. About 3 per cent. tin is obtained by the process.

UTILIZING NICKEL WASTE.

To utilize the waste from nickel sand, which collects on the bottom of vats and also from cast nickel anodes, wash same often in clean hot water and then boil in dilute sulphuric acid, in which there is 1 part of acid and parts of water until the water, when poured upon waste, does not cloud same any more. At this stage pour off the liquid and submit the waste to treatment with concentrated nitric acid. Great care should be taken in doing this, a large earthen vessel being used to prevent the solution from running over. The solution will be of sufficient concentration when it contains but little free acid and should then be filtered and slowly evaporated, until dry, over the water bath. The name of the resultant product is nickel-nitrate. Proceed by the dissolution of this nickel-nitrate in hot water and precipitate same with gradual additions of caustic soda. Then filter and wash this precipitation of hydrated nickel oxide and submit it to treatment with dilute sulphuric acid with the assistance of heat until its solution. Concentrate this solution by evaporation and add an excess of concentrated solution of ammonium-sulphate. This precipitation is a double solution of nickel and ammonia and can be used for nickel-plating.

VARNISH—ASPHALT, FOR SHEET METALS.

A bright asphalt varnish for sheet metals is made by boiling cold tar until it shows a disposition to become hard, when it gets cool. This can be found out by rubbing a little on a piece of metal. Twenty per cent. of lump asphalt is then to be added to the tar and stirred in until the lumps are melted. Then it is allowed to cool and can be kept for use.

VARNISH—BLACK, FOR IRON WORK.

For making black varnish that has a gloss, fuse three pounds Egyptian asphaltum; when it is liquid add one-half pound shellac and one gallon turpentine.

VARNISH—BLACK, FOR STEEL AND IRON.

A black varnish for steel and iron is made by boiling together sulphur and turpentine. Upon evaporation of the turpentine a thin layer of sulphur is left, which is united with the iron when heated a short time over a gas or spirit flame.

(2) For a good black varnish for covering iron work, etc., use 48 pounds of asphaltum; add 10 gallons of boiled oil, red lead and litharge 7 pounds each, dried and powdered white copperas 3 pounds. Boil for 2 hours; then add 8 pounds dark gum amber (fuse), 2 gallons hot linseed oil; boil for two hours longer or until a little of the mess when cooled may be rolled into pills, then withdraw the heat, and afterward thin down with 30 gallons of oil of turpentine.

VARNISH—BLACK, FOR STOVES.

To make a brilliant black varnish for stoves and fire-places, ivory black stirred into ordinary shellac varnish is said to answer the purpose well.

VARNISH—BLACK, FOR TIN.

An excellent black varnish for zinc or tin is composed as follows: Equal parts of chlorate of potassium and blue vitriol (sulphate of copper) are dissolved in 36 times as much warm water, and the solution is allowed to cool. If the sulphate of copper contains iron, it is precipitated as a hydrate oxide, and can be removed by decanting or filtering. The metal pieces to be coated are then immersed in the solution, or the solution may be flowed on, and allowed to remain a few moments, until the metal becomes black. Then rinse off with water and let dry. Even before it is dry the black coating adheres to the article, so that it may be wiped with a cloth. If copper-colored spots appear during the operation, the same solution should be applied a second time in the same manner. On rubbing, the coating acquires a glittering blue appearance, like indigo, but this disappears on applying a few drops of linseed oil, varnish, or "wax-milk," and the metal then has a deep black color and gloss. The "wax-milk" above referred to may be prepared by boiling 1 part yellow soap and 5 parts Japanese wax in 21 parts of water until the soap dissolves. When cold it has the consistency of a salve, and will keep in a closed vessel for an indefinite time. It can be used for polishing carved wood and for waxing ball-room floors, as it is cheaper than the solution of wax and turpentine, and does not stick or have any disagreeable odor.

VARNISH—BLACK, FOR ZINC.

A black varnish for zinc is made by the dissolution equal parts of blue vitriol and chlorate of potash in 36 times their volume of warm water. The solution is then permitted to cool. Should there be iron in the blue vitriol it is precipitated as a hydrated oxide and its removal can be made by filtration. Next, plunge the zinc castings in this solution for a second or so, when they will become very black. Then rinse them off in water and dry them. This black coating will adhere to the article even before it is completely dried. The solution should be applied a second time should copper-colored spots make their appearance during the operation. If you rub it, a glittering appearance, something like indigo, will be acquired by the coating. This, however, will disappear on the application of a few drops of Linseed Oil Varnish, which is composed by boiling together 5 parts of Japanese wax and 1 part of yellow soap in 21 parts of water, until the dissolution of the soap. The zinc, after being treated with this varnish, has a deep black color and gloss.

VARNISH—COLOR, FOR SHEET METALS.

A color varnish for sheet metals is made by powdering 7½ drachms of acetate of copper in a mortar, spreading this powder in a thin layer upon a plate and allowing it to stand in a lukewarm place. In the course of a day or two the evaporation of most of the acetic acid and water of crystallization will have taken place. The residue of light brown powder is then to be triturated with oil of turpentine, into which there are stirred 3½ ounces of high-grade fat copal varnish of a heat of 1.67 degrees Fahrenheit. If the rubbing of the acetate of copper has been thoroughly performed the dissolution of most of it will be evaporated after 15 minutes' stirring. Then pour the varnish into a glass bottle, put it in a warm place and shake it often. The little amount of acetate of copper settling on the bottom can be used again for other portions of varnish. The color of this varnish is a dark green, and it takes 4 to 5 coats to produce a brilliant green luster on sheet metals. If a gold shade is desired 2 coats are sufficient. The article to be gilded being heated in a drying chamber or upon metal-plates which have been uniformly heated. The time of heating is the determinent of the resultant shade, which may be either green or yellow, dark yellow, orange or reddish-brown.

VARNISH—COPAL.

Copal varnish is made as follows: Pale African copal, 7 pounds; fuse; add clarified linseed oil, one-half gallon; boil for 5 minutes. Remove it into the open air, and add boiling oil of turpentine, 3 gallons; mix well; strain it into the cistern and cover it up immediately. This is used to varnish furniture, and by japanners, coachmakers, etc. Dries in 15 minutes, and may be polished as soon as hard.

VARNISH FOR COATING WOOD AND IRON.

A good varnish for coating wood and iron is made by placing 3 pounds powdered resin in a receptacle, adding to same 2½ pints spirits of turpentine, shaking well and allowing same to stand, shaking from time to time, for two days. After the elapse of two days, 5 quarts of boiled linseed oil are to be added, and the whole shaken together. Then decant the clear portion, reducing same with spirits of turpentine, in order to acquire the right consistency.

VARNISH FOR DECORATING TINPLATE.

Rub to a fine powder 30 parts of crystallized acetate of copper, and leave it in a thin layer on porcelain for a few days in a moderately warm place, to drive off the water of crystallization and a portion of the acetic acid. Rub the bright brown powder that is left with a small quantity of turpentine, and add it with constant stirring to one hundred parts of fine copal varnish heated to 167 degrees F. If the acetic acid was sufficiently finely powdered, it will dissolve on stirring it about a quarter of an hour. Pour the varnish into a glass vessel and set aside for a few days, with occasional shaking. The varnish is dark green. Four or five applicotions to tinned iron give a fine green, lustrous tint. If heat is applied two coats will give greenish, yellow, dark yellow, orange, or reddish brown tints, according to the temperature. The source of heat may be an oven or an equally heated iron plate. Success depends on the uniform application of the varnish and the heat.

VARNISH FOR IRON.

A varnish for iron is made by mixing, when warmed in an iron kettle, ½ pound powdered resin, ½ pound asphalt and 2 pounds tar oil. The mixture must be dissolved and care must be taken to prevent any contact of same with the flame.

VARNISH FOR IRON PATTERNS.

A varnish for iron patterns is made by dropping strong sulphuric acid drop by drop into oil of turpentine. This will cause a precipitation in the oil of turpentine of a syrupy nature. The acid should be added until the precipitation no longer forms. The liquid is then poured out and the syrup washed, when it is ready for application. The iron to be varnished is to be heated to a luke-warm heat and after the application of the varnish allowed to dry.

VARNISH FOR POLISHED EDGES.

White lava varnish is used to preserve polished edges from rusting and at the same time not detract from their appearance. Also white varnish may be used; or dissolve as much white resin in one-half pint of turpentine as it will take, and apply with a paint brush.

VARNISH FOR MACHINERY.

A varnish for machinery and foundry patterns, which dries as soon as put on, gives the patterns a smooth surface, thus insuring an easy slip out of the mold, prevents the patterns from warping, shrinking or swelling, and is quite impervious to moisture, is prepared in the following manner: Thirty pounds of shellac, 10 pounds Manila copal, and 10 pounds of Zanzibar copal are placed in a vessel which is heated externally by steam, and stirred during 4 to 6 hours, after which 150 parts of the finest potato spirit are added, and the whole heated during four hours to 87 degrees C. This liquid is dyed by the addition of orange color, and can then be used for painting the patterns. When used for painting and glazing machinery it consists of 35 pounds of shellac, 5 pounds of Manila copal, 10 pounds Zanzibar copal and 150 pounds of spirit.

VARNISH FOR TINPLATE.

A receipt for varnishes for tinplate is as follows: Take 30 grams of sub-acetate of copper (copper green) and make into powder, spread quite thin on a porcelain plate and keep in a moderately warm place for some days. After this time, the crystal water and the greater part of the acetic acid will have evaporated. The light-brown powder that remains is then ground in a mortar with some turpentine and 100 grams of fine fat copal lac warmed to 167 degrees F., is then added. If the copper oxide has been well prepared it will be mostly dissolved after a quarter of an hour's stirring. The varnish is then put in a glass and kept in a warm place for some days, keeping occasionally stirred. The small quantities of acetate of copper, which are still deposited, are used in the next preparation. The dark green varnish gives a fine glittering color on tin, but only after the fourth or fifth coating, but two coatings will give the most varied colors after drying in a drying chamber or on warm iron plates. Greenish, yellowish, or dark-yellow gold colors, then orange, and, finally, reddish-brown shades are obtained, according to the duration of the temperature. The colors are far brighter than those obtained by English gold lac, and keep fast under light. The composition of the gold color depends on the deduction of the dissolved copper oxide into the hydrosilicate of copper, which is soluble in small quantities as gold color in the copal lac. The more deduction is obtained the darker the colors will be.

VARNISH—GREEN, FOR METALS.

Thoroughly dissolve in a strong potash lye a quantity of finely pulverized gum sandarac. This solution is to be diluted with water, and then follows its precipitation with a copper salt solution, either acetate or sulphur. Wash and dry the green precipitation, which is then dissolved in oil of turpentine.

VARNISH—GREEN TRANSPARENT.

A green transparent varnish for metals is made by grinding a quantity of finely-powdered chromate of potash with one-half the quantity of Chinese blue, to which is added a sufficient amount of copal varnish, thinned with turpentine. If the alteration of the tone of the varnish is desired, the amount of the various ingredients used should be changed accordingly.

VARNISH—METAL.

A good varnish for metals is made by decomposing potash or soda soap with sulphate of zinc. This soap is then purified by water, and after 10 per cent. of tallow has been added the mass is diluted by petroleum, which affects the dissolution of the metal soap. The compound is then filtered until it is bright and clear.

VARNISH TO PREVENT RUST IN IRON AND STEEL.

Dissolve 1 part white wax in 15 parts benzine, and apply a thin layer with a brush. This forms a perfect covering, and is easily removed when necessary.

VERDIGRIS.

Verdigris is made from either copper and vinegar, or by putting together sheets of copper with the skins of pressed grapes.

WAGNER'S BRITANNIA METAL.

Wagner's Britannia metal is composed of

83-100 parts Bismuth,
3 6-10 parts Zinc,
81 1-100 parts Copper,
9 66-100 parts Antimony,
85 64-100 parts Tin.

WARNE'S METAL.

Warne's metal is composed of

7 parts Nickel,
7 parts Bismuth,
3 parts Cobalt,
10 parts Tin.

This metal is white.

WASHING BRASS WITH TIN.

To wash brass with tin, boil together 6 pounds of cream of tartar, 4 gallons of water, and 8 gallons of grain tin or tin shavings, for half an hour in a porcelain-lined vessel; put clean brass ware in the boiling liquid for a few minutes, or until properly coated.

WELDING CAST-STEEL.

In welding cast-steel it should be kept from the air during the heating and should be heated as quickly as possible. It should not be made too hot or it is liable to either burn or break in pieces while being hammered.

Coke, not coal, should be used for the fire, as the latter contains sulphur, which would give the surface of the steel a sulphide or iron coating. The following is the flux to use:

¼ pound Washing Potash,
¼ pound Borax,

and a small quantity of white glass, powdered. These ingredients being mixed together, and, when cold, powdered. This flux will accomplish the dissolution of oxide formations. Before the steel is placed in the fire apply some to protect the surface of the work from oxide.

(2) A welding compound that is excellent for cast-steel is composed of

3 to 5	parts	Carbonate of Soda,
15 5-10 to 26 7-10	parts	Ferro-cyanide of Potash,
35	parts	Common Salt,
7 6-10	parts	Resin,
41 5-10	parts	Boric Acid.

WELDING COMPOUND FOR STEEL TO STEEL.

A compound for welding steel to steel is composed of

10 parts Borax,
2 parts Sal-ammoniac,
1 part Flour of Sulphur.

Another for the same purpose is composed of

8	parts	Calcined Soda,
15 5-10	parts	Prussiate of Potash,
35	parts	Common Salt,
41 5-10	parts	Boric Acid,

WELDING COPPER.

The ingredients of a mixture for welding copper are

2 parts Boric Acid,
1 part Soda Phosphate.

WELDING STEEL TO STEEL.

The following compound is useful for welding steel to iron or steel:

35 parts Iron Filings (free from rust).
70 parts Sal-ammoniac,
70 parts Prussiate of Potash,
500 parts Borax.

This compound is to be pulverized in a mortar and next turned into a crucible. Water is added until a thick paste is made and the crucible is put over a wood fire and the contents are continuously stirred. The resultant is then cooled, pulverized, and is ready for use. It looks a good deal like pumice-stone, with green and gray streaks.

WELDING WROUGHT IRON AND STEEL—COMPOUND FOR.

A compound for welding wrought iron and steel, at a red heat, is composed of

7 6-10 parts Colophony,
26 7-10 parts Prussiate of Potash,
35 parts Boric Acid,
30 1-10 parts Common Salt.

Another compound is composed of the following mixture:

6 parts Borax,
1 part Prussiate of Potash,
½ part Resin,
2 parts Sal-ammoniac,

pulverized and mixed with water. The mixture is then boiled with constant stirring until the formation of a stiff paste. This paste is then hardened over a fire, and, when cold, pulverized and mixed with 1 part wrought iron filings, free from rust. In use the powder should be scattered upon the red-hot pieces and liquefied over the fire.

WELDING WROUGHT IRON TO WROUGHT IRON AT A RED HEAT.

A compound for welding wrought iron to wrought iron at a red heat is composed of

½ part Sal-ammoniac,
½ part Water,
1 part Borax.

These ingredients are boiled and stirred until stiff, then they are allowed to harden over a fire. After it is cooled the compound should be pulverized and thoroughly mixed with 1-3 part of unrusted wrought iron. Dovetail the pieces to be welded and make the place to be welded red-hot, then scatter the powder upon it and liquefy over a fire. A light tap or two with a hammer is ample for joining the pieces together.

WHITE METAL.

White metal is composed of

42 parts Tin,
40 parts Lead,
2 parts Cupro-manganese,
20 parts Antimony.

WHITENING BRASS AND COPPER.

The whitening of brass and copper articles can be accomplished by boiling them in a solution of 1 pound grained tin, ¾ pound cream of tartar and 2 quarts water. The dissolution of tin takes place in the cream of tartar, and it is again precipitated on the brass and copper.

WHITEWASH THAT WILL STICK AND WASH.

For a wash which can be applied to lime walls and afterward become waterproof so as to bear washing. Take 3 parts silicious rock (quartz), 3 parts broken marble and sandstone, also 2 parts of burned porcelain clay, with 2 parts freshly slacked lime, still warm. In this way a wash is made which forms a silicate if often wetted, and becomes after a time almost like stone. The four constituents mixed together form the ground color to which any pigment that can be used with lime is added. It is applied quite thickly to the wall or other surface, let dry one day, and the next day frequently covered with water, which makes it water-proof. This wash can be cleansed with water without losing any of its color; on the contrary, each time it gets harder, so that it can even be brushed, while its porosity makes it look soft. The wash or calcimine can be used for ordinary purposes as well as for the finest painting. A so-called fresco surface can be prepared with it in the dry way.

WRINGER ROLLS.

To put on new rolls, wind the shaft, after old roll has been removed, with jute twine. Place one end of the shaft in a vise and cover the shaft with a thin coat of rubber cement, twist the new roll on as quickly as possible, and let it stand two or three days before using.

WRINGER ROLLS—CLOTHES.

For manufacturing rubber rolls for clothes wringers, the vulcanized rubber in sheets is rolled tightly around the iron cores. The material being cohesive or adhesive, sticks together. The roller is then put into an iron mold and pressed tightly, so that the iron core or spindle will be forced to the center. The whole is then put in the steam oven and vulcanized. Rubber cement is used for mending old work. It may be had from rubber dealers.

ZINC COVERED IRON PLATES.

For covering iron plates with zinc, first see that the plates are thoroughly cleaned; then dip them into a bath of chlorides of zinc and ammonium, and finally in a bath of zinc and mercury.

ZINC-NICKEL.

Zinc-nickel is an alloy composed of 90 parts zinc and 10 parts nickel, used as a pigment.

ZINC OXIDE.

Zinc oxide is made by burning zinc white.

ZINC SULPHATE.

Zinc sulphate is made by roasting blende and lixiviating the mass with water.

INDEX.

A

B

C

D

E

F

G

H

I

J

K

L

M

N

O

P

Q

R

S

T

U

V

W

Y

Z

Important

We make as large a variety of modern cook stoves, ranges and heating stoves as can be found in the assortment of any manufacturer in the United States.

Our business, in every department, is conducted on economical rather than on extravagant lines, from which the dealer derives the benefit, as we charge only a very moderate profit above absolute manufacturing costs, for our best as well as for our lowest priced productions.

Channon=Emery Stove Co., Quincy, Illinois.

They Save Fuel

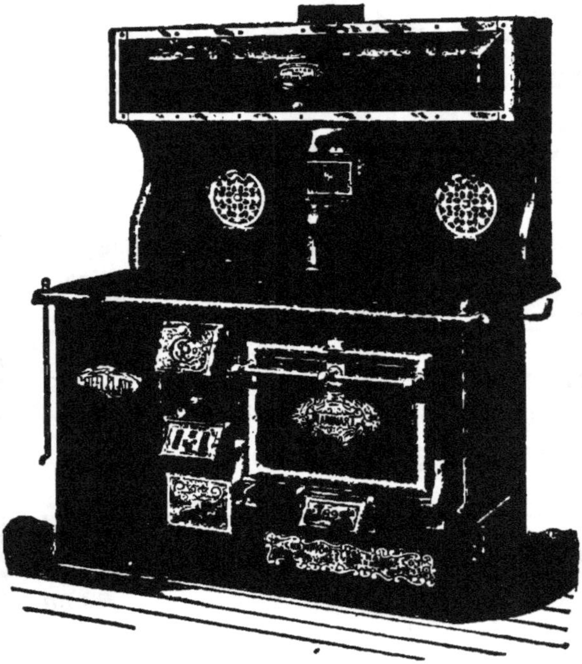

That is the foundation of the great popularity of the

Champion and Marquart
STEEL RANGES

THE BEST MADE, OWING TO THEIR DOUBLE FLUE CONSTRUCTION.

It will pay you to control the best line of steel ranges, made in all styles and sizes, before your competitor gets the agency. Write now.

CHAMPION STEEL RANGE CO.,

251-257 Viaduct, Cleveland, Ohio.

CHICAGO STOVE & RANGE CO., Chicago, Western Agents.

www.ingramcontent.com/pod-product-compliance
Lightning Source LLC
Chambersburg PA
CBHW020850270326
41928CB00006B/642
* 9 7 8 3 3 3 7 2 1 7 8 9 1 *